I0461990

How to
EXPLAIN BITCOIN
to your mum

by
Jason Deane

Copyright © 2018 Jason Deane

ISBN: 978-0-244-73409-1

All rights reserved, including the right to reproduce this book, or portions thereof in any form. No part of this text may be reproduced, transmitted, downloaded, decompiled, reverse engineered, or stored, in any form or introduced into any information storage and retrieval system, in any form or by any means, whether electronic or mechanical without the express written permission of the author.

PublishNation

www.publishnation.co.uk

To my nan, a truly wonderful lady who had absolutely no idea about technology.

And to my mum, who has continued that tradition.

With love

How to explain Bitcoin to your mum

Introduction

I genuinely wrote this book for my mum.

I thought if I could actually make my mum understand what Bitcoin is, then it would be possible for absolutely anyone – and I mean ANYONE – to understand it and how it will form such an important part of the financial world going forward.

I should point out that I don't mean any disrespect to my mum, she's worked hard through her whole life and done well for herself, but I'm sure she's the first to agree that she definitely isn't technical. This is a lady who spent years telling people I worked at 'Microwave' instead of a large Seattle based software company. She doesn't have the internet, can't understand why people would use it, and has only recently acquired a mobile phone. Not a smartphone you understand, a phone that only makes and receives phone calls - and does nothing else - on a Pay-as-You-Go system. Not that she's ever made any calls on it as her initial credit expired, completely unused, after 90 days and she has no idea how to top it up. She's never received any calls on it either as she keeps it switched off to save the battery, making actually contacting her on it rather tricky. Nevertheless, she has one, and that's good enough for her.

As you can see, I may have bitten off more than I can chew, but if there's one thing my mum will tell you, it's that I like a challenge.

This book is written, really, for that audience of one. Whilst writing, I have imagined myself reading each section of it to my mum, using concepts she will be familiar with and *not* using buzzwords or technical acronyms she definitely won't be familiar with. This means, of course, if you, or someone you know, is really struggling with this whole concept of what Bitcoin is (or even those other 'coins' you sometimes hear about), or you just need to check your understanding at a basic level, this may well also be the book for you.

I would ask my mum if she minds you reading it too, but I can't get hold of her on her mobile right now.

I'll send her a letter instead, but in the meantime, let's assume it'll be fine.

Chapter 1
You're overcomplicating it.

"Life is simple, but we insist on making it complicated"

– Confucius

It's probably logical that I start with my own 'Bitcoin' story and how I managed to make sense of this whole, crazy thing.

Some of what follows may surprise you when you consider where I am in the industry now, but, like everyone, I had to start at the beginning and learn the ropes. The fact is I really didn't do this very well and I managed to get myself completely confused over the whole thing more than once. This may sound very scary if you're reading this hoping to get a clear understanding of it all only to find that the author – a proud and self-proclaimed nerd – had trouble too. However, bear with me, because the reasons for this are peculiar to my case and also due to my haste to try and run before I could walk, as we'll see.

The problem for me when starting out on this journey into 'cryptocurrency' was actually the same as it is for everyone else – I still needed someone to explain it to me in very simple terms to start with. And I mean REALLY simple terms, using the sort of words you'd use to explain it to a child of about eight years old. So, in short, <u>not</u> words like 'cryptocurrency' that I have just casually thrown into the start of this paragraph without thinking. I needed easy words I could understand, immediately recognize, and feel comfortable with, such as 'money' or 'payment' or 'bank account.'

The trouble was, I just couldn't find anyone who was willing to explain it that simply when searching for articles on the net. Those articles tended to be very technical (which I just didn't understand), badly written opinion pieces (the content of which irritated me as much as the bad writing) or lots of people shouting 'scam' who, I later realized, had even less understanding of it all than I did. It was enough to put me off or confuse me, and whilst it succeeded completely in the latter, it didn't quite succeed in the former, although it made me question (for a while) what I was even doing in this apparently 'dangerous' new environment.

5

However, in my case, I'd had some experience of that feeling of confusion and I drew on that to muddle through and find the understanding I needed. You see, some twenty-five years earlier, I had been working at Microsoft as this new concept of 'the internet' had started to unfold and the early confusion about understanding it was also quite prevalent. It felt *exactly* the same this time as it did then. And of course, in those days, there was no internet to look up information about, well, 'the internet', so asking around was the only way forward. This meant exposing yourself in a high tech environment as not knowing the answer, but it also meant getting an answer from someone who didn't really know either. Incorrect information was common and speculation ran abound. It seemed a couple of decades later we were back at the same point, just the subject in question that had changed.

So whilst this proves that even someone with a technical background can get this wrong if they start in the wrong place or with the wrong assumptions, I can categorically assure you that this doesn't have to be the case. Whether speaking at events or just talking to people one-on-one about Bitcoin I always use the analogy of driving a car, and it's worth remembering this as you work your way through this book. Let me explain:

Remember when you started driving? It was exciting, scary and, at the time, seemed very difficult. There was so much to do: find the biting point on the clutch, release the handbrake, move forward, check surroundings, check mirror, depress clutch, change gear, release clutch, indicate, check mirror again and so on. Then there was the constant decision making: who gives way to who, which way to turn at complex intersections and thousands of others. We made all of these decisions consciously at this point, checking and questioning each one as we did so.

Fast forward a few years, and you'll run out to the car one morning, late for work, with a slice of toast in your mouth, throw the coat you're carrying on the passenger seat, slam it into gear with the clutch pushed in whilst starting the engine to save time, drive out in reverse probably a bit too fast whilst simultaneously putting on your seatbelt, and find your spot in the traffic as you listen to the radio and finish that toast - all without any conscious thought at all. It's second nature now, isn't it?

And yet most of us do all this without really knowing how that car actually *works*. We just turn the key or press the button, and it goes. Sure, you know it's something to do with tiny explosions in some chamber somewhere pushing pistons or something, but I bet you don't know the firing order of the cylinders, or what the correct tappet settings are. If I asked you to take the engine apart and rebuild it, most of us would politely decline – the task would seem overwhelming. Many of us, in fact, aren't that interested anyway. But we all still drive these complex machines around, don't we?

This is very much like using and understanding Bitcoin. You can, if you wish, go on a course to understand what's going on 'under the hood.' You can delve into the technical background, analyze the code and learn how to – metaphorically speaking – change the oil. But you simply don't *need* to. All most of us want is for someone to show us how to drive the car, in a patient way and in simple terms, *not* take it apart to discuss where each piece goes in enormous, complex detail. This is where this book comes in. To put it in terms of the car analogy, it's designed to show you how to drive, talk about why it's good to do so and explain the Highway Code. It won't tell you how to fork an existing open source coin and create a new proof-of-work algorithm. Which is just as well because I'm not really sure how to do that anyway.

So let's close the bonnet, step back away from the car and start with the basics.

Chapter 2
We fear change, especially when it comes to money.

"Never doubt that a small group of thoughtful, committed, citizens can change the world. Indeed, it is the only thing that ever has"

– **Margaret Mead**, American cultural anthropologist

Bitcoin is money, pure and simple, it's just in a different form to what we're used to as it *only* exists in a digital format. As incredible as it may seem, it's just another step in an evolution that's been going on for years - centuries in fact - and each time a whole generation has had to get used to a new form of money which then becomes natural for the generation that follows. It will be no different this time around and this new form of money is no more alien to us as other previous changes to financial systems were to our predecessors.

That's a bold statement, but let's consider the history and what we, as people, have already had to get used to and look for any patterns in the changes that came about. To do this, we'll need to do a bit of a history lesson. Bear with me, this will make sense as we go through.

As far back as there have been humans, there has been money or trade of some sort and in the beginning there was only one system available - bartering. This was complicated, time-consuming and relied on finding what economists refer to as a 'coincidence of needs'.

For example, let's assume we have two gentlemen who live in the same ancient village; Mr. Smith is a farmer who has fields of potatoes and Mr. Jones keeps livestock in the form of chickens and sheep. They both agree that 20 potatoes equal one chicken and swap at regular intervals. However, Mr. Smith would like a sheep as well, but Mr. Jones simply doesn't need that many potatoes, so doesn't want to trade. However, Mr. Smith could exchange some potatoes with Mrs. Miggins who is offering a very nice shovel that Mr. Jones is sure to like. So, after some discussion about what items are worth what, he swaps the potatoes for the shovel with Mrs. Miggins and then offers the shovel to Mr. Jones in exchange for a sheep. Phew.

But even this simplifies the issue. What if Mr. Jones doesn't want the shovel or doesn't think it's worth a whole sheep? What if Mr. Doyle from the other side of the village wants to swap his cabbages for potatoes? What if Mr. Doyle thinks his cabbages are worth TWO sheep? Who sets the values? And who wants to go through this every time you want to get an item you don't produce yourself? We must also consider the human element and the - somewhat rougher – times these people lived in. Everyone was looking for an edge, perhaps giving away a sheep with a hidden sickness, or handing over just slightly fewer potatoes than was agreed and so on. We can presume that people who knew each other well would probably have an element of trust between them as there was a need for inter-dependence, but what about people who were from other towns? This may not end well for them! Trust was fragile. In many ways, it still is, there are just better systems to spot those who would look to abuse it.

The barter system probably ran in some form or another for thousands of years, but as time went by, a whole new concept of exchange started to appear - gold and other precious metals. Not everyone might want a new shovel, but the vast majority of people would be happy to have a solid gold nugget, its value apparently universally accepted very early on. After all, it is very scarce, relatively easy to transport, desirable to all and could be used to show status and importance.

But this just shifted the problem to another point in the chain of transactions. How much gold is a sheep worth? What if my nugget is too big or small to buy it? How will we make the trade fair? And, the biggest of them all, how will all the people who have been bartering all their lives now deal with this crazy new idea of using one medium of exchange for all transactions?

"What happened to good old fashioned bartering?" people will say.

I can't help thinking there must have been people, even then, saying "it'll never work" and "it's a scam" before, inevitably, they had to join the rest of the community who had already adopted this new 'gold system'.

As time went by, new problems arose. Why use real gold when you could use counterfeit gold? A piece of lead dipped in gold would be almost indistinguishable from the real thing and a con artist could do very well for himself, as long as he moved on before he was rumbled. What was needed was some way to identify the gold was real and this came in the form of markings made by an official body, usually a government or a monarchy of some sort, effectively giving its official 'approval' to a gold piece and making it unlikely it was counterfeit. It was often easier to flatten the gold into small circular pieces or different sizes to make this marking process easier and thus, the coin was born. If gold was being offered without the approved markings on it, it may not be accepted or its value may be disputed, so, in theory, the system was robust.

However, this system still falls foul of our rather imperfect human selves. Being the central controlling power meant that coins could be manufactured with less of the precious metal in it than there should have been by using cheaper substitutes, keeping the precious element for other purposes, but still with the official seal in place. This was neatly demonstrated in the ancient Roman Empire where silver coins that were issued at the end of its reign contained almost no actual silver at all in an attempt to reduce the cost of the vast armies it needed to maintain order. But that raises another question – if it is still accepted by people as being official, does that actually matter? The coins in your pocket have far less value in pure metallic terms than they have in the markings they carry, yet this doesn't bother us in the slightest. At one time in history, however, that was unheard of.

Of course, those who had got used to the 'chunk of gold' system might not like this at all, and the ones who were still frantically hanging on to the bartering system *definitely* wouldn't know what to make of it. An 'official' coin? You can imagine them getting together and making comments like "it'll never work" and "it's a scam" before, inevitably, joining the rest of the community when the benefits became obvious. We humans are incredibly sceptical and resistant to change where it concerns money, so adoption takes time. It always has and it always will.

What happened next seems like a natural evolution to us from the vantage point of looking back into history, but at the time this was an enormous change and I have no doubt met with extreme scepticism. Coins, it appears, had some issues and limitations and more refinements were needed.

The problem was that since there were no banks, no safes and no secure houses as such, if you had coins you had to keep them with you at all times. If you were rich and had a lot of them, this was quite a challenge. It also made you a target for thieves, pickpockets and all manner of dishonesty. For traders and merchants, the issue was even more severe. If you were buying, for example, a full ship's cargo of silks to sell in another land, the cost might be many hundreds, or even thousands, of copper, bronze, silver or gold coins. How do you carry that sort of weight? How do you protect it, even from your own crew who are prone to temptation?

This prompted the first known instance of paper money, which is thought to have originated in China during the Tang Dynasty, somewhere around the 9th century. The thinking was that instead of, say, 1000 copper coins being carried and exchanged for a transaction, an official paper note stating that the owner of that note could exchange it for those 1000 copper coins could be made and given instead. The recipient of the note would, on his next trip to the capital, pay a small fee and exchange the note for his coins which would then be released to him from an 'official' central repository. Of course, once the confidence in the notes rose amongst merchants, an obvious shortcut presented itself. Why bother going to the capital each time to claim the coins – why not just trade with the notes themselves? In other words, the notes were considered as good as the coins amongst the traders who used them. It should be noted that this 'flying cash' (as it was often referred to due its tendency to be blown away in the slightest wind) was really only originally designed for merchants and not really end users like you and me, but the idea was set. However, it wasn't until around the tenth century during the Song Dynasty that paper notes were expanded to the public at large and became legal tender, using a similar basis as before.

However, the resistance this would have encountered must have been substantial at first. Imagine yourself as a merchant with a large supply of very valuable spices or silks that you were selling to a wholesaler. You would be handing over your entire livelihood for a single piece of paper. As you can imagine, those who had always traded with pieces of gold or physical coins would be seriously worried about this at first and almost certainly wouldn't have just taken someone's word for it. Remember, there was no internet, no communications network and no newspapers to spread the word of a new financial development. It must have taken months, or even years, for these notes to have been universally accepted amongst the "it'll never work, what's wrong with good old fashioned gold coins/gold pieces/bartering" brigade. And I bet you anything there were a group of people who viewed it with extreme suspicion and considered it a scam.

By somewhere around the seventeenth century, most countries were producing notes to represent coins. Usually, these were backed by a central government controlled depositary, and bearers of the notes were always able to take them to the central bank and exchange them for the gold (or other precious metal) equivalent. By now, all sorts of financial instruments had evolved, such as early forms of bonds and shares, but this didn't usually affect the average man in the street as these were out of the reach of most of them. But something interesting was happening with debt and this led to the next great financial change.

There have always been debtors and creditors. From the very early days of 'tally sticks' (a medieval English system whereby amounts owed were represented as notches on a debtor's stick that could only be matched up with the same notches on the creditor's stick) to 'charge plates' used in America in the 1800's to extend credit to farmers until harvests came in, there has always been debt management of some sort. In the early 1900's, also in the USA, some local banks, department stores and oil companies started issuing an early form of credit card, initially designed to build customer loyalty to specific groups. But in 1950, Diner's Club launched the world's first 'universal' credit card, an idea which was developed quickly by other companies. Easy, instant credit was available!

But, again, this presents a whole new set of problems. Imagine you're running a traditional motel out west and a family arrives to take a room for the night. Instead of cash, they offer you a small piece of plastic to pay with - a piece of plastic that you can't even keep! You've never seen this before, but they assure you that by writing down the numbers on it and filling in a form, a company you've never heard of will send you the money for their bill. It sounds as ludicrous as accepting a piece of paper instead of coins did hundreds of years previously. As usual, there was resistance from certain quarters with the familiar cry of "it'll never work" or "it's a scam" and "whatever happened to using good old-fashioned notes/gold coins/ gold pieces/the bartering system?" Some things never change, do they?

The rate of change in money, however, has accelerated rapidly in the last fifty years in particular. Once the gold standard had been abandoned by most countries (in the simplest terms, this is the idea that all 'notes' are backed by physical gold held in a central reserve) new forms of monetary policy could be developed leading to all sorts of solutions as well as new problems. Digital money started to evolve and this was another giant leap that was difficult for many people to adapt to. Even as late as the 1970's many people were still being paid in cash at the end of the week by companies. On Friday afternoons workers would literally line up in a designated area of the business they worked for and receive their week's wages in cash, known as the 'pay packet'. This was only forty years ago and it already seems completely absurd! With the advent of early computer systems and new, more modern bank accounts, however, people could receive their pay in cheque form (another piece of paper!) or even, a bit later, paid directly into their accounts in digital form. Can you imagine THAT leap if you were one of the people collecting your pay from the office every Friday? Instead of having physical hard cash in your hand, you'd instead get a different piece of paper that told you that you'd received some 'virtual' numbers in some 'virtual' bank account, neither of which you could actually physically touch and both of which you had to rely on someone else to make work, i.e., the bank and the company you worked for. How could it possibly be real?

Inevitably, there were people who were not happy with this or regarded it with extreme suspicion. Those familiar cries of "it'll never work" or "they're trying to scam us" or "what's wrong with good old fashioned cheque/notes/gold coins/gold pieces/the bartering system etc. etc.?" echoed in grumbled tones around works canteens the country over as the changes were implemented. Well, ok, maybe they didn't mention gold coin, gold pieces or the bartering system in the 1970's, but you get the gist.

To be fair, this last change was probably the biggest one in terms of leaps of faith by the average person. Until then, there had always been some *physical* representation of money, it was just the format it was in that was in question. But now, for the first time in history, there was only a 'digital' representation, just numbers on a screen or on a printout. Of course, you could still turn it into the cash that you recognized by joining the lunchtime bank queue on a Friday. It had to be lunchtime because ATMs were not yet in use and banks were only open for what seemed like a few minutes a day from Monday to Friday. How things have changed.

If you think about it, this is all about having confidence in 'the system' as a whole. When the whole concept of just getting your money in 'digital' format first came about, there were a lot of unknowns and a lot of concern about what would happen when something went wrong, as it always does at some point. These days, of course, whatever we think of bankers and their role in the world, you can't really disagree that the system that runs in the background allowing us to transfer money, use ATMs, access our accounts via smartphone or tablet etc. is pretty solid most of the time. In fact, it's even possible to live without using cash at all without any real inconvenience. You receive your salary as a digital number in your virtual account, and you use plastic (or an app on your phone) to pay for each and every purchase, even the small ones which can be done instantly and easily using contactless technology. In other words, it's all digital. And, as every day goes past, the world is going more and more digital and with even traditionally cash-based devices such as car park ticket and snack vending machines accepting cards or phone payments. Cash is becoming obsolete, except perhaps in the world of crime where not being traceable is still a very important benefit of using it.

When you consider all of this, the concept of Bitcoin suddenly doesn't seem to be such a leap, does it? In some ways, it's the exact same thing as the digital money we're already used to in that it only exists on a screen somewhere. You can even take it out of your account and spend it in your local currency if you want to. But there *are* many differences and it's probably those differences that are causing you the concern, at least it was in my case.

As we've already seen many times over though, change can often take a while to be adopted, and the more radical the change, the greater the initial resistance. Right now, in 2018 when this book is being written, adoption (and understanding) is low in relative terms, whilst resistance and suspicion run high. No one knows exactly how long it will take for these positions to reverse, but they probably will at some point for reasons we will see later on.

At the moment, however, all we need to do is get an understanding of it so we're ready. So let's take a look at what it actually is and how (on a non-technical level) it works.

Chapter 3
What even is a 'Bitcoin' anyway?

"At its core, bitcoin is a smart currency, designed by very forward-thinking engineers. It eliminates the need for banks, gets rid of credit card fees, currency exchange fees, money transfer fees, and reduces the need for lawyers in transitions... all good things."

– Peter Diamandis, Founder and chairman of the X Prize Foundation

Before we delve into what this new financial concept is, I'm going to make an admission, even at the risk of exposing myself to great ridicule.

I remember reading my very first article on Bitcoin on the train coming from Reading station one afternoon somewhere in 2013 I think. It was fascinating, even though the article was very much written with the assumption that the reader already knew what Bitcoin was. I didn't at the time, I'd never heard of it, but I immediately knew I wanted to know more.

Sadly, I had made one critical and embarrassing mistake – I had misread this new alien word of 'Bitcoin' as 'Britcoin' with an 'r' in it, as in 'Britpop' or 'Britannia.' And once you've created a new association in your mind that a word is written or pronounced in a certain way, your brain always sees it like that until either an outside influence forces you to look at it again (in other words, someone pointing out your mistake whilst laughing at you) or you have one of those "hang on a minute ..." experiences. For me, it was the latter, but I think I must have been about twenty articles in before I spotted it. Not a great start.

So, if you're still worried that you won't be able to understand it, I think we can put that fear to bed at this point. At least you can read the word right.

So, how to explain Bitcoin? Well, in the simplest terms, it is a brand new currency. In the same way governments came together and created a new currency out of thin air called the Euro in 1999 for the member states of the European Union, this currency has also been created out of thin air as, in fact, *all* currencies really are if you look at them closely. The difference is that this time there's no central government involved in setting it up and there's no physical coins and notes you can actually see – it only exists in digital format the same way the money you have in the bank only exists in digital format. (Those pictures of bitcoin notes and coins that you may have seen adorning news articles are actually just made for images, they don't really exist in any real form) Of course, the digital 'non-existent' money you have in your bank account can be drawn down into cash and spent in shops, or, as we've already discussed, spent via plastic. It may surprise you to know that Bitcoin can also be spent in the same way, it's just not as mainstream or as easy to do yet.

As soon as you understand that Bitcoin is just a currency, it all starts to make sense. If you were going on holiday to France, you'd find a Bureau de Change and swap your pounds for Euros before you went, wouldn't you? This is no different. At any point, you can swap your pounds for Bitcoin, or vice versa, by paying in or out of your bank account on specific websites. It's true to say this process is a bit of a hassle at the moment as the technology is still 'clunky', but the basic idea is exactly the same. But here's where it gets interesting.

The Euro was the first attempt at getting a currency that is universally accepted across a swathe of countries, 19 at the last count. When you consider that there are around 195 countries worldwide (technical definitions can make the number vary between 193 and 196 depending on which one you apply), this means almost 10% of the world's countries will now accept one currency. The great thing about this is when you travel around Europe you can take and use all the same notes and coins with you as you travel – you no longer have to keep buying local currencies as you change countries like we did before 1999. Trade between the countries is also much easier as everyone can immediately understand the value of the monetary unit you are using. There are certainly problems with it, not least the fact that each country's economy is different and removing control of monetary policy at a local level can be dangerous, but the idea is a noble one.

Now, imagine if we expanded this idea a bit and we had a currency that could be used *anywhere* around the world at any time and would be accepted by *everyone*. Even better, this currency would not require the governments of countries to give up their local monetary policies. You can send money to anyone in the world almost instantly at very low cost, use it to buy any product or service and you wouldn't need to go to a bank or even have access to any bank account whatsoever - a tap of your finger on a smartphone or a computer keyboard would do the job. That is the mission of Bitcoin.

This, of course, is revolutionary, but you could argue that parts of this have successfully been done before. We've come close to a global currency with gold as we can assume everyone, or at least nearly everyone, will accept it. You don't need a bank account to transact with gold and it could be traded independently of each country's monetary position. But you can't send it instantly around the world and you're still exposed to the problems of keeping wealth in this format safe as we've already seen. In fact, sending money anywhere in the world is still really problematic even with today's technology.

It still astounds me that we can video conference someone on the space station from our phones, but we can't easily send money to different parts of the world. Yes, there ARE some services that allow certain transactions such as PayPal, Western Union type services and the good old-fashioned bank transfer, but they are either slow, expensive, have low limits or are difficult to use. The reality is that if you wanted to send a big chunk of money from London to New York, the quickest way to do it would be to jump on a plane yourself with the cash in a bag next to you. That's ridiculous in this day and age and if, like me, the first time you heard that you thought that it just couldn't be true, I'd encourage you to look into it a bit. It really is the case. We live in an increasingly connected and digital world, with instant communication, information and access to anything we want, but our money system has not yet caught up. Bitcoin was created, partly at least, as a solution to that – a digital currency for an increasingly digital world.

We'll learn more about where Bitcoin gets its value, who owns and manages it and where it came from in due course, but for now, let's deal with another word that made an appearance early on this book and has yet to be explained - cryptocurrency.

The 'currency' bit is now clear having made the comparison with money units we already understand and are used to, but what is the 'crypto' part about, and how does it differ from Bitcoin?

This is one of those things that sound really complicated at first but is actually quite simple when broken down. It's all very well having a global currency that is independent of any banking system or any single government, but how, then, do you make it secure? As we've seen from the history lesson earlier, we humans can be pretty mean to each other when it comes to money, and there has always been a certain percentage of the human race who will literally stop at nothing to make themselves rich, usually at the expense of others. We all know that coins and notes can be, and have been, copied and passed off as originals to unsuspecting souls, even with the modern anti-counterfeit checks in place, but that doesn't apply here. The beauty of using ONLY computer code rather than any physical objects to represent your currency – in this case Bitcoin – is that you can set a level of security in the code so high that there is not enough computing power on the planet to break it. Right now, there isn't, and there probably won't be for a very, very long time.

I promised I wouldn't get technical so I have no intention of explaining how that works behind the scenes, except to say that the whole premise is based on 'cryptography', the purest definition of which is "a method of storing and transmitting data in a particular form so that only those for whom it is intended can read and process it."

In other words, when I send Bitcoin to you, the transaction is done in such a way that it is a mathematical certainty that it will arrive as much as it is a mathematical certainty that it will not be intercepted, stolen, duplicated or in any other way compromised on the way. It's all in the code, written by some very smart people with big foreheads, and it uses a very advanced and unbreakable form of cryptography to do it. This is one of those examples of something we don't need to know in detail, or even at all, to use it, but it does show where the word comes from. 'Cryptography Currency' sounds a bit long and cumbersome, but shorten the word, squash the two together and 'Cryptocurrency' has a ring to it, doesn't it?

There ARE other cryptocurrencies of course as this is a generic term for any currency that uses this system (or a close variation thereof), and we'll touch on those later, but there is only one Bitcoin, and it was first on the scene.

Incidentally, the underlying security behind the wizard's curtain that makes Bitcoin so incredibly secure is really quite remarkable. Bitcoin has been around since 2009 and it remains the only currency that has ever existed that has never been compromised in any way. But that doesn't mean we've solved the problem of us humans still being nasty to each other, it's just moved it somewhere else along the chain.

To give you an example, consider the way that car security has changed over the years. Right up until around ten or fifteen years ago, car theft was common. All a thief needed to do was break in, hook up some wires and drive off. As technology got better, this got harder and harder and, eventually, it got to a point where it was next to impossible to steal a car without the keys. It would be lovely to say that the problem was then solved, but the reality is it just forced the thieves to change tactics. Now, instead of breaking into the car, they simply break into the house to steal the keys for the car and *then* drive off with it! We'll never win the battle against the bad guys, but we'll certainly make it as hard as we can for them. That means even with Bitcoin, you still need to keep an eye out for people trying to get it as it is, after all, just another currency.

Bitcoins HAVE been lost, but mostly by the carelessness of the owner - a bit like losing a wad of cash on a drunken night out. But there are some bad guys who have successfully stolen people's 'keys' or hacked exchanges (the digital version of the Bureau de Change where you buy your Bitcoin) where they are stored, a bit like a digital bank robbery. Of course, all payment systems or mediums of exchange are subject to those problems, and always have been, but Bitcoin still has the advantage because the actual coins themselves cannot be compromised like other currencies.

It still ain't perfect, but it's the closest we've ever come and that, in itself, is also revolutionary.

Chapter 4

Who started Bitcoin and who's running it now?

"It feels strange to think of a world without cash, no more coins or notes for us to find down the back of the sofa ... but it appears that's the way things are heading."

– Sir Richard Branson, Founder of Virgin Group

This is where the story takes an unexpected turn. The simplest answer to the first part of this question, i.e., who started it, is, well, we're not quite sure.

I should clarify this a bit. We know who most of the people who worked on the code are, we know where and when a lot of the work was done, but we don't really know the person who masterminded the project and wrote the document that outlines the visions and plan for the currency, known as the 'white paper'. We only know he, she or they (it's possible it's a group) identified themselves as "Satoshi Nakamoto" during the development stage before signing off and disappearing for good. No-one knows what he/she/they looked like or where he/she/they are now. (I'll stick to 'him' for now based purely on the masculinity of the name or these sentences will get too long otherwise) But there's also another twist in the tale.

When you use, store or buy Bitcoin, you first create a 'wallet' to do so. A 'wallet' is a word used to describe the Bitcoin version of a bank account and you can log in at any time from anywhere to see the balance or move it around, in a very similar way to online banking. Setting up a wallet is actually no harder than setting up a new email address since all the clever stuff has been done in the background by the guys with the big foreheads again and we don't need to concern ourselves about how it all works. It just does.

However, it's actually possible to see the contents of everyone's wallets on a public ledger if you were interested. Whilst that may sound like a very scary prospect, I should add that it is impossible to identify whose is whose in reality as each wallet is only shown as a long and complicated string of random numbers and letters. This, in fact, is how it is possible to use Bitcoin relatively anonymously, but we'll learn more about what that actually means later. So, although you can see all the balances for everyone's wallets, you can't tell who they actually belong to. It might be interesting in the same way it would be interesting to have a nose into everyone's bank accounts, but it doesn't really tell us anything since we'd expect to see all balances from nothing to lots, and everything in-between anyway.

That said, there is one wallet that we can be almost entirely certain about for various technical reasons; it is the one that belongs to the mysterious Satoshi Nakamoto himself. At the same time that Satoshi disappeared in 2011, the wallet fell dormant and has never been used. Astonishingly, it still contains 980,000 Bitcoins which were worth $19.5 BILLION during the last peak in December 2017. This would make Nakamoto one of the richest people in the world, and yet he has never touched it.

Many attempts have been made to find Satoshi Nakamoto to no avail, although clues to his identity have been found in his posting patterns, writing style and within the code itself. People have also come forward to claim that they are the mysterious creator, but all have so far been disproved. Whatever the story, it seems that anonymity and silence suits him. For now.

Economists do, however, hold a concern over the Bitcoins that are currently locked up in Nakamoto's wallet. For reasons that we will learn later, there is a total limit of 21,000,000 that will ever exist due to a hard cap built into the code, i.e. there's a mathematical ceiling built in that cannot be amended by anyone. This means that this one wallet holds around 4.7% of (what will be) the entire circulating supply of coins, which means in turn that one person could significantly influence the value of the coin, at least in the short term, by dumping them all on the market at once. Should Bitcoin become the global currency some think it will be, that could be enough to create a period of instability.

To put that into context, the country with the most gold in the world is the USA, with around 4% of the world's total reserves. It's theoretically possible, therefore, assuming Bitcoin becomes a truly global currency, that one person could control more of the world's currency than the US government currently does in terms of global gold reserves. That's a staggering thought.

However, this doesn't actually matter at all in terms of how Bitcoin works, operate or develops on a day to day basis, because the code that runs in the background and makes it possible for us to use and spend Bitcoin is 'open source'. In short, that means it's in the public domain and anyone can see, access it, change it or even make their own coin with it (perhaps calling it 'BRitcoin!'). This may sound like it goes against the security aspects we covered earlier, but actually changing the code doesn't mean your changes will be implemented because they definitely won't. The global network that runs and support the Bitcoin system will simply reject everything that isn't in the exact structure that it recognizes. As soon as you change even one tiny aspect of it, it is no longer recognized and will be universally and instantly rejected. I'm simplifying a little there to keep my promise of not getting technical, but that's not too far off how it works.

What this means is that the network is secure and self-governing. But changes *have* been made, improvements added and the network expanded, so, if you can't make the changes yourself, who owns it and is making them happen? Who is responsible? Can they be corrupted? Who, exactly, are we trusting with our wealth here?

That 'open source' part I mentioned earlier is the key and this is one area I need to go into in a bit of detail. Don't worry though, we're still not going to get technical.

You don't need to understand computer code to understand 'open source' but you might need an example to get an idea of the key differences that apply here, so let's take the example of two programmers, Mr. Geek, and Mr. Nerd.

Mr. Geek writes a new program that he wants to sell to make money. This is fair enough as he has worked hard to create it and needs to make a living, so he is rewarded by receiving an income from each unit he sells. However, only he has access to the code and the law protects him from would-be intellectual property thieves who would look to capitalize on it. He is solely responsible for the program and if any problems are identified with it, he must fix them himself and send out any updates or fixes and may even be liable for any damages that it may cause to someone's computer. When you download an app that you pay for on your phone, it is almost certainly an example of this 'closed source' code. You will not be allowed to share it or play with its code in any way. Microsoft Office on the computer I'm using right now to type this also follows the same rules.

Mr. Nerd, however, has a different agenda. He has an idea that he wants to share with the world, but he understands that although he is a good programmer, having many good programmers work on the problem would be much better and will find and solve more problems than he ever could on his own. So, he releases his initial code to the public, perhaps with a 'white paper' explaining his ideas, and invites other people to tinker with the code and help him. Changes are tested by lots of different people rather than one and then implemented or dropped according to the agreement, or 'consensus,' of the group as a whole. These programmers may never receive any direct payment for the work they do, but they may benefit in other ways as the project progresses.

Bitcoin, as you've probably already guessed, falls into the latter camp. Once Nakamoto released his initial ideas into the wild, some 30,000 lines of excellent code by all accounts, everyone was able to work on it, improve it and find problems with it. This last part, in particular, is very important because open source projects tend to be more secure than closed source versions. In our example above, Mr. Geek could, if he wanted to, insert some hidden malicious code into his program that does something nasty to your computer when you run it, but with an open source project this is all but impossible as someone would spot it and remove it before it became part of the final version. This is, again, slightly simplified, but it gives us a good enough understanding of how the system works.

The Bitcoin that we know today is run by a large collection of people who have an interest in seeing the project work. In theory, they can be anyone as everyone can propose changes, but they tend to be developers who understand the code and the bigger picture and want to ensure that it works today and going forward. That said, no changes can be implemented unless ALL participants agree, i.e. a consensus is reached. This is both the advantage and disadvantage of a purely demographic system; on the one hand, no-one can force through changes that are bad for the project or strong arm people into submission for their own ideas, but on the other, this can delay the implementation of good ideas while consensus is being reached. This criticism aside, it is clear from progress thus far the model works and, on the whole, works very well.

It's important to understand that this is a different question from 'who OWNS Bitcoin' because the answer to that is quite simply 'nobody and everybody.' Nobody owns Bitcoin any more than anybody owns the technology that makes email work and that is actually quite a good analogy: We wouldn't want our email to be controlled by a central body because it would be far too easy for it to be compromised and far too tempting for governments and their agencies to monitor it. In the same way, we really don't want our financial transactions being controlled through a central body because it forces us to trust that central body to manage that transaction properly for us. The banks that we use in the traditional financial model of money don't exactly have a good track record of 'trust' so removing them from the control of this system is generally regarded as a good thing by Bitcoin enthusiasts.

Importantly, it's also not controlled by any government, financial institution or company, all of whom would have their own agenda and almost certainly end up either destroying it or warping it into something that no longer resembles what it was designed for. Even better, the bigger the network gets – and it is already truly global – the lower the chance there is for any such organization to take significant control in any form. It is almost certainly too late for that to ever happen, even at this early stage. Bitcoin is sometimes described as a "currency for the people, by the people" and whilst this is slightly Utopian in some ways, it's not without merit. And anyway, it sounds cool.

In short, no-one owns Bitcoin, there is no 'Bitcoin Incorporated' and no-one can stop it from developing or unfolding as long as people choose to use it. It would be like trying to stop the internet itself – since there is no central point, this is all but impossible and even countries that impose severe restrictions like China or North Korea cannot keep it out completely or indefinitely.

No, Bitcoin is truly independent of any race, nationality, colour, creed, social status or political and financial power.

Bitcoin, quite simply, is here to stay.

Chapter 5

Where did Bitcoin come from?

"Every informed person needs to know about Bitcoin because it might be one of the world's most important developments... Bitcoin might revolutionize more than money or economics. It could transform the role and nature of government."

– Leon Louw, Nobel Peace Prize Nominee

We'll either first hear about Bitcoin through a friend or through an article of some sort, but the usual assumption (as in my own case) is that it is a very new phenomenon, literally just out of the box. The reality, however, is that it's older than you probably think.

Don't get me wrong, there's no question it's a new technology and it has a long way to grow and develop, but it's actually already over a decade old. Yes, Bitcoin is older than your smartphone. Well, except possibly my mum's.

It was in August 2008 that the website 'Bitcoin.org' was first registered and a few months later that the mysterious Satoshi Nakamoto published his white paper called "Bitcoin: A Peer-to-Peer Electronic Cash System." It was here he outlined his vision of a new currency that would be accepted around the world without the need for central banking systems. These are all facts that are quite well known and getting more detail on them on the internet is easy to do. However, it's also worth asking the question: *why?*

Let's take a minute to remember what was going on in 2008. The world had just witnessed the 'credit crunch'. Huge, century-old institutions had failed, ordinary people had seen their savings wiped out and hundreds of thousands more lost their jobs and homes. As bad as it was, it soon became clear that many players in the giant, complex banking system hadn't exactly been playing by the rules in their pursuit of bonuses and inflated profits. The world was shocked and people were disillusioned not only with the banks who had been blatantly fraudulent in some cases, but also the politicians who had been turning a blind eye for their own political gain. Worse, very few of the people who had been perpetrating these unprecedented levels of corruption were actually punished for it. As a result, there was a very powerful 'anti-establishment' feeling in the air and it became a perfect breeding ground for a new generation of geeky activists called 'cypherpunks'.

A cypherpunk is a name given to someone who is looking to create social and political change through the use of cryptography or another privacy-based process to 'beat the system' of what they see as an incredible invasion of privacy by big business and, especially, governments. OK, that sounds long and complicated when I read it back, but basically it means that they want to create technology that can be used without worrying about who's listening or watching.

Wherever you stand on this argument, you have to admit they have a point. Our data, our internet activity, our whereabouts and our image are now routinely monitored and stored without our direct consent all the time. Governments and commercial organizations know more about you than you ever thought possible, even if, like my mum, you don't use any modern technology. For example, if you just went shopping one lazy afternoon, your image will be stored on dozens of CCTV cameras, the car park will log your number plate and the financial organizations will report back to the retail organizations that you spend £5.80 on cat food at the Co-Op in Tunbridge Wells at 2.13pm precisely. These companies love it because it means they can sell us more stuff and governments love it because they know exactly what you're up to and how you're likely to vote in the next election. And that's just the tip of the iceberg.

The problem with new technology is that it can be used and manipulated according to the agenda of the person doing the manipulation and this has always been the case, going right back to the very first technological breakthroughs. Take fire, for instance. You can use it to provide warmth and a way of cooking food for families, or you can destroy whole cities with it. Today we face the same thing, just on a much more complex level. What is needed instead is a completely 'trustless' system because one thing we've learned from history is that we humans are rubbish at keeping our word or abiding by laws when it comes to money or technology, especially humans in power. Incidentally, that word - trustless – is an important one and we'll keep coming back to it in various forms as we progress.

In this context, you can see what the cypherpunks wanted to do, i.e. use technology in a way that disrupts that process of information gathering or snooping but without necessarily compromising all the cool stuff you can do with technology. Why not be able to make phone calls without agencies listening to them? Or send emails without them being intercepted? Or even just go somewhere without being constantly tracked, you know, like we did for the first 99.99999% of mankind's entire existence?

Of course, this leads to the classic, ongoing argument of personal freedom vs control of the bad guys, and I don't propose to resolve it here. What is important is that what little trust there had been in the establishment at the time had been lost and the motivation of this group was, as a result, exponentially increased. After all, if the status quo was quite happy to do this to their own people, then the people needed a choice.

What would be ideal, so the thinking went, was a form of money that was independent of the 'corrupt' central powers that controlled it. Money that couldn't be devalued at the whim of a government because they'd made a terrible economic decision. Money that couldn't be seized in a bank account. Money that could be transferred instantly, at low cost, without having to tell anyone or clear it with them first. Money that could be sent across the world regardless of sanctions or central agreements. Money that couldn't necessarily be traced by governments or other agencies. Money that could be sent safely to people that you didn't even necessarily trust. Money that could not be stopped by anyone, *ever*, so long as the people wanted it. That would really disrupt the establishment, wouldn't it?

In the midst of all this angst and idealism, Satoshi's Nakamoto's white paper about a new currency proposal was first received by the cypherpunks. The timing, really, was perfect. There had actually been a few attempts previously at creating a purely digital currency, one even as early as 1982, but all had failed due to a lack of interest or, more commonly, a lack of technology. It was as good an idea as it had ever been, but timing is an essential ingredient to make anything work. In the words of Victor Hugo, nothing is as powerful as an idea whose time has come and this time the world was ready AND the technology was in place. It was now a question of making sure it worked.

As Nakamoto pressed the 'enter' key on his keyboard for the first time on January 3rd 2009 to run his program beginning the process creating Bitcoins, it speaks volumes that hidden deep in the code was a single line of text that simply read:

"The Times 03/Jan/2009 Chancellor on brink of second bailout for banks"

It served no purpose, it added no value, wouldn't affect the running of the computer code and would only ever be seen by the few people who were geeky enough to be able to read the code, but I think it's no coincidence that of all the comments he could have added, he chose to put in a line that highlighted the collapsing establishment, as he may well have seen it. Talk about 'sticking it to the man!'

But of course, this was only the beginning. It's all very well creating some very clever code that 'magics up' some monetary units from – literally - nowhere, but how on earth does it get any value? Why would anyone in their right mind want to have it when you can have dollars or pounds? And where did all these Bitcoins come from anyway?

Well, to understand that bit, we need to look under the hood just a tiny weeny bit. Don't worry, it's no more than a glance really. And I do mean the same kind of glance you would give to an engine of a second-hand car you were buying.

After all, you just *have* to open the bonnet and have a look even if you have no idea how any of it works, don't you?!

Chapter 6

How Bitcoin actually works

"When I first heard about Bitcoin, I thought it was impossible. How can you have a purely digital currency? Can't I just copy your hard drive and have your bitcoins? I didn't understand how that could be done, and then I looked into it and it was brilliant."

– Jeff Garzik, Co-Founder of Bloq Inc, Bitcoin developer

So far we've learned what a Bitcoin actually is and how and why it came about, which is all very nice, but it has probably raised more questions than it answers. The most obvious one is how on earth it made the leap from being a bit of computer code on Satoshi Nakamoto's computer to being a medium of exchange around the world. In December 2017, a single Bitcoin was worth almost $20,000 on the open market and now that you know what its origins were it seems even more unlikely – crazy even – that this could happen.

But there is really simple, yet genius, logic behind all of this. In short, it's pure economics and maths, and those clever, big-brained cypherpunks I was telling you about figured out how to link the two things together.

Most of us know about supply and demand. That is, the lower the supply something has relative to the demand for it, the more value it has. Gold, for example, has a high demand and a low supply, so it always has value as long as that ratio stays that way. Leaves on the trees in my garden have high supply but low demand, so I'm not likely to become a millionaire anytime soon selling them. It's a simple, age-old premise that forms the basis of pretty much everything in the financial markets, except where governments come in and start fiddling with things, that is. The bottom line is that something is only ever worth what someone is willing to pay for it, and this applies to literally everything, including Bitcoin.

Those first few Bitcoins Nakamoto created early in 2009 had no real value at that time. There would only have been a handful of people who would have been even able to accept it and they were probably involved in the project anyway. But these people knew they were building something long term, so that wasn't an issue. But outside of this little community, Bitcoin was subject to the same rules of supply and demand as everything else so had to fit the bill and have a 'value'.

The secret is in the code and the network it uses to run. It's complex, clever and way, way beyond what we need to go into here, but there are a few bits of cleverness we can extract and talk about in plain English, and so we shall.

The first is the network that supports how Bitcoin works. In the old days, when you wanted to build a network that did something (like a phone system or a company database that runs over several sites or countries) you had to build it yourself, or more likely hire a big company like IBM to do it all for you. You'd need to buy all the computers, all the software and even, in some cases, the cables that joined it all up. You'd then need to pay clever people with clipboards and coloured pen lids poking out of their shirt top pockets large salaries at each location to make it work and maintain it. You can see why computing was such an enormous investment for organizations, and still is in many cases.

This would never work in the post-cypherpunk world that Bitcoin wanted to operate it in because it would mean that someone would own the network and therefore own Bitcoin. Before it had even started, it would be dead in the water and would have completely failed in its idealistic objectives. No, what was needed was a system whereby literally *anyone* could be part of the network and be rewarded for doing so. There would be total freedom so that anyone could join it or leave it and any time they wanted without having to tell anyone or agree on it first. Even those big, bad, corrupt organizations could be part of it if they wished, but they'd never be able to control it, no matter how they tried. Everyone, of course, would be paid in the very Bitcoin they were helping to support in the first place, according to how much work they put in.

Of course, questions you might be asking are 'why would you need a network anyway?' and 'What is it supposed to do?' and both are natural responses to what you've just learned. They can both be answered by looking at what Bitcoin was trying to achieve.

WARNING: This is the most technical bit in the entire book. Grab a cup of tea, relax, take a deep breath and let's go for it!

Let's say I am a total Bitcoin enthusiast. I am, of course, but let's pretend we're back in 2010 and the project has only been running for a year. The concept behind it has attracted quite a lot of attention and already thousands of (mainly very technical people) are now wanting to get involved, even if it's just out of curiosity. Let's say you want some Bitcoin and I have some kept safely in my wallet (that's the Bitcoin version of a bank account) on my computer that I can send to you. You'd create a wallet like mine (a simple install, like putting an app on your phone), and I'd send it over to you, almost exactly like sending an email – both, after all, are just bits of code at the end of the day. Within a short time, the amount of Bitcoin you asked for, minus a small fee for sending it, has arrived in your wallet. But how?

Remember that network we talked about earlier? Each person who has volunteered to help with that network is making the act of moving that one Bitcoin from me to you happen, not just one or two of them, you understand, ALL of them. If more joined tomorrow and we did it again, all of THEM would be helping too. In fact, the bigger that network is, the more computing power that joins it, the more secure it is as they would ALL be involved. But how on earth does this make sense?

How this works is also *why* Bitcoin is so secure. When I send that Bitcoin to you, every single computer on the network, whether owned by a black, white, male, female, old, young, rich or poor person must agree that it has been sent by me and received by you. This is done by everyone on that network running a program that talks to everyone else, but with each one independently working out the answer to the 'secret code' of making that transaction work. Remember, we're talking about clever maths and cryptography, the art of encoding information, so someone has to figure out the next step in the code to allow the transaction to happen. When someone does, that computer lets all the other computers know what the code is and they confirm it (it's easy when you know what the answer is) and put it in a record, a copy of which is then transmitted and kept on every single participating computer. This means, of course, that no one person can tamper with the record as it won't match up with all the logs on the other computers and will be rejected if you try. Accessing all those independent machines at the same time would be nigh on impossible to do, so the network remains extremely secure.

The transaction is then classed as verified and the Bitcoin passes from me to you. The computers, which run 24 hours a day, seven days a week, simply move on to the next transaction. The person who found the code is then rewarded with some newly created Bitcoin according to what the program is set to give out at that time.

This means, of course, that only the person who actually found the 'secret code' actually gets rewarded, and everyone else, although participating, gets nothing. The act of working like this is a bit like traditional gold mining if you think about it. You could be working in your mine for weeks or months and not find a thing. Then, one morning you strike gold in a big way and get your pay off. This analogy has not been lost on the people who provide all the processing power for the Bitcoin network and they actually refer to themselves as 'miners'. It's a very different interpretation of the word, but you really can't argue with the logic.

This is not exactly how the whole thing works, but it's pretty close and if we go any further we're in danger of getting into real technical detail which I promised we'd avoid. You can stop gripping that teacup now, we're now at the end of the 'technical bit'!

If you think this sounds complicated, imagine writing the software that runs all of this. Frankly, even though I am technically minded, I wouldn't know where to start. The good thing is, as users, we don't really need to know the ins and outs (like driving that car we talked about earlier), but understanding this helps to understand where the value comes from.

And, if you really didn't get that, please don't worry. In the end, it won't make any difference when using it. The key point is that the way the program works makes sure that creating Bitcoin can only be done in one very specific and controlled way i.e., that is offering up processing power and electricity, whilst being entirely governed by a fully automated and totally secure program. It can't be copied, made up on a whim or forged, you have to either earn it, buy it, or trade goods and services for it, the same as any other currency. This means that Bitcoin has a limited supply, one part of the economic requirements for value, although it still needs a demand for the equation to be complete.

Of course, the astute among you may have spotted a few problems with this to do with managing supply. If we're giving out new Bitcoins all the time, won't the world eventually be full (in a virtual sense) of Bitcoin all over the place? Surely we'll have hard drives full of it and we'll need 100 billion of them to make the tiniest transaction? No. This also, as it turns out, has been thought of in advance.

You see, as the network becomes more powerful, it would, in theory, get easier and easier to find the next 'secret code' to make each transaction work. Because it's a sort of race to get the answer first, we have seen a proliferation of more and more powerful machines being produced, dedicated only to the pursuit of Bitcoin. Companies and individuals have sunk millions and millions and millions of dollars into it in an attempt to be the first person to find the code and get the rewards each time. This means the power of the network as a whole has grown exponentially, but the rate at which the number of Bitcoin being created has remained exactly the same. How is this possible?

Satoshi Nakamoto thought of this and considered it inevitable that this would happen. That clever little piece of code not only runs the whole Bitcoin structure, it also constantly adjusts how hard it is to find the next 'secret code' using mathematics according to how much power is in the network. If you add a really powerful machine, it will go up dramatically to compensate for the increased computer power. If you turn most of them off, it will drop dramatically. Whatever the power in the network, the code makes sure that new Bitcoin will never be produced at the rate of a fixed amount every ten minutes. And there's even a second layer designed to slow down production as time goes on.

Right now, you are rewarded with 12.5 new Bitcoins if you are the first to find the secret code, but it wasn't always this amount. When it started, the reward was 50 Bitcoins. They were easy to get and they required very little processing power, but they were also worthless as there was such a tiny community interested in them. Four years later, exactly as the program was designed to do, the reward dropped to 25 coins to reflect the growth in the network. It then dropped again to 12.5 coins – the current level – and in May 2020, it will drop again to 6.25 coins and so on, every four years, in a process known as 'halving'. Eventually, the amount of reward will be tiny, just a few fractions of a Bitcoin, and the processing power to obtain them will be exponentially higher than it is now. That brings us to the third control to ensure that Bitcoin will never suffer from inflation like all other currencies – there is a finite amount that can ever be produced.

Yes, the code has one more trick up its sleeve: it will stop new Bitcoin being produced when it reaches its maximum of 21,000,000. Again, because we're dealing with the absolute certainty of mathematics, we know that the last Bitcoin will not be produced until 2140, some 132 years after Nakamoto hit that return key on his computer for the first time. Now THAT'S foresight.

If you happen to be around at that time, rest assured that Bitcoin will continue to run and exist exactly as before, but no more Bitcoin would ever be produced. Miners would simply be paid the transaction cost instead.

So now we know that we have a controlled supply and nothing can affect that supply, how do we account for the demand that gives it the value the marketplace says it has? Who exactly, to be more precise, is actually using it? We'll examine this in the next chapter.

And we won't be doing it using any technical details. You deserve a break.

Chapter 7

How Bitcoin has Value - *Part 1*
Supply

"Economists and journalists often get caught up in this question: Why does Bitcoin have value? Bitcoin [has] value because it is useful and scarce."

– Erik Voorhees, CEO, Shapeshift

We find ourselves dealing with basic economics again to answer this question, right back to the supply and demand question. We've already seen that supply is an absolute number, so logic tells us that there must be some sort of demand for Bitcoin if its price has risen even slightly above zero in terms of money we recognize, like dollars or pounds, which it quite clearly has. However, before we move on to that, there's still a little more to learn about supply that may not be immediately obvious.

So far, as of October 2018, we have mined around 82% of the total supply of Bitcoin that will ever exist, that's some 17.3m coins. The last four million coins will take another 122 years as the exponential effect of the halving really takes hold, but most of them will still be done by around 2026. This is not many in reality. There's not even enough for every millionaire in the world to own one, let alone us 'normal' folk. However, the supply situation is even worse than that.

Whilst Bitcoin can only be created by the processes we have seen, it can, unfortunately, be lost, destroyed or permanently locked away by literally anyone. You'd have to buy it first of course, so it would be a very expensive thing to do, but it's your right once you own it. It's no different to withdrawing £500 from the cashpoint and throwing it in the fire when you get home. It's your money after all, you can do what you want with it, but in practice not many people do this as far as I know.

However, whilst the cash is replaceable (the Royal Mint has produced millions more just while you've been reading this book), Bitcoin isn't. Once it's gone, it's gone. Forever. This means, over time, the supply will get even scarcer than it is now.

Last year, in late 2017, a digital forensics firm called Chainalysis, estimated that somewhere between 2.78 and 3.79 million Bitcoins have already been lost forever, so somewhere between 13% and

18% of the entire supply. This means, in reality, there will never actually be more than 17.21m – 18.22m Bitcoin in circulation and not the 21m there's supposed to be. That's enough to give one Bitcoin to every man, woman and child in Kazakhstan, but that's all. There's just not enough to go around.

It's important to keep reminding yourself that this is designed to be a borderless, global currency. That means it doesn't matter where you live in the world or what sort of government system you are living under, you are, technically, eligible to use it. In pure numbers, it means that 7.5 billion people are able to use and trade with Bitcoin, but there'll only ever be around 18 million coins in circulation. That's only 0.0024 Bitcoin each, assuming no more are lost or the world's population doesn't keep increasing over the next 122 years, both of which seem unlikely.

As you've probably guessed by now, this had also been considered by Satoshi Nakamoto. Bitcoins can be traded right down to eight decimal places, i.e., as small as 0.0000001, which is one hundred millionth of a Bitcoin. However, it's a bit of a mouthful to say

"that'll be nought point nought nought nought nought nought nought nought one Bitcoin please"

in the same way it would be a mouthful to say

"that will be nought point nought one pounds please"

if we were buying something for a penny.

So, like we have 'pence' as a portion of pounds and 'cents' for dollars, we needed a word for the tiny fractions of Bitcoin that made up the whole, so the word 'Satoshi' was chosen in honour of its creator. So instead of stuttering out a long line of noughts in the example above, we'd say "that'll be one Satoshi please". Traders sometimes shorten it to 'Sats', but it means the same thing. The reality is, should Bitcoin become as globally accepted as many people think it will, most of us common folk will only be dealing in Satoshi – only the very, very rich would be able to have an entire Bitcoin to themselves. They would, in theory, be worth millions or even billions of dollars (assuming that dollars still exist at that point.)

I should add that although there are many people, like myself, who firmly believe that Bitcoin will go mainstream and become a truly global force, there are probably just as many who think it won't and I would certainly agree it's not a given that this will happen. We'll come back to this point later when we look at what the future holds for Bitcoin, but for now and *only* for the purposes of this book, we're going to assume that it will.

Going back to the issue of supply, we surely need to examine how on earth all these coins got lost. At the time of writing this book (October 2018) this lost Bitcoin amounts to an incredible value of up to $24.64 BILLION. How could people have been so careless? If you knew you had a winning lottery ticket that was worth a few billion, or even a few million, you'd probably take very good care of it, wouldn't you? It's very unlikely you'd scrunch it up and stick it in your jacket pocket somewhere with a bunch of receipts, and yet it seems some people have actually done this, albeit in a virtual sense.

The answer is, of course, most of this happened in the early days when Bitcoin had no real value. Bitcoin was easy to mine as the network was tiny and you could even do it on a very basic laptop and get several Bitcoin a week. The trouble is when something is as easy to get as Bitcoin was in those days, it doesn't really have a value unless you're really forward-looking and understand that you need to hold on to it for a few years.

To a certain extent, this applies to everything. You can pick pretty much any household item around you, bury it in the ground for a few hundred years and it becomes priceless by virtue of its rarity and novelty. The timescale is different, and we're only talking in a virtual rather than physical sense, but the process is the same. Bitcoins were as common as pencils back then, about as easy to get and as expensive to buy, so you'd probably take care of one about as much as you take care of a pencil. Consequently, many people didn't. I mean, if you realized that you'd left one of your pencils in Argos when you were filling out one of those little slips, would you be bothered enough to go back and get it? What if it was worth £10,000?

I personally know of people who mined Bitcoin in the early days because it was a novelty and a really cool, geeky thing to do. They mined a few coins, saw the whole lot was worth just a few pence and then couldn't be bothered to go through all the effort to sell them, especially since at the time it was all a bit of a hassle to do. Over time they changed their computers or lost the hard drive and the coins were lost forever. And 'lost' really does mean 'lost.' If we burn our money it can be replaced. If a ship sinks with a ton of gold bullion on board, it's possible that it could be retrieved one day in the future when salvage technology is better. But Bitcoin can never be recovered. It's like a deleting a file permanently, formatting the hard drive it was on, blowing it up with dynamite and sending all the parts to different planets. It ain't coming back from that.

Perhaps the most famous incident of this happening is James Howells' story. He had been mining Bitcoin in the early days and claimed to have amassed around 7,500 coins by 2013. Sensibly, he'd realized that Bitcoin might be worth something one day, so took out the hard drive of his machine and put it safely in a drawer. Somehow, either through confusion or carelessness, this hard drive was thrown away and ended up buried in a landfill site somewhere in England. Those Bitcoin today would be worth around $48,000,000. It was an expensive mistake.

But it wasn't unique. Campbell Simpson in Australia also accidentally threw away a hard drive with 1,400 Bitcoins on it, worth a not-insignificant $9,100,000 at today's prices. Undoubtedly, this will have happened dozens or even hundreds of times in the early days of Bitcoin before people really understood what they were worth and started taking care of them. Whilst I'm sure it'll happen again, the actual number of Bitcoin will be much smaller and the frequency will be, and already is, far lower. Remember that lottery ticket example? Now you KNOW for certain it has high value, you'll be guarding it with your life, not leaving it lying around where it can be accidentally thrown away.

These accidents seem to imply that it's easy to 'just lose' Bitcoin, but I should clarify this a little. Bitcoin is designed to be pretty robust. If something goes wrong on your computer or the smartphone you're using, it is always possible to retrieve your Bitcoin, easily, instantly and completely free of charge, from that central 'ledger' or 'record' stored on all the computers we talked about earlier, a bit like restoring an accidentally deleted email, or, to go even more 'analogue', rescuing a thrown away document from the bin outside your house.

To do this, all you need is your 'private key' (either a long string of characters and numbers or a unique twelve-word phrase) that is linked directly with the Bitcoin you have on that ledger, like a beefed-up password. All you need to do is enter that private key and you'll get your Bitcoin back.

The problem in the examples given above is that the hard drives these people threw away actually contained not only the Bitcoins, which were recoverable, but also the private keys, which were not. Had they even just written the keys down on a piece of paper, it would never have been a problem. This is also why, as the value of Bitcoin has continued to grow and the user interfaces with wallets have got easier and easier, fewer and fewer incidences of this are happening.

That said, it will still be many years before the issue goes away forever, if at all. Now that we have had Bitcoin in existence for a whole decade, it's been long enough to find new problems. There have, for example, already been incidences where people who owned Bitcoin have died and not left the private keys where anyone can find them. One of the few advantages of a central system, such as a global bank, is that you can go to them when sorting out someone's estate with a death certificate and follow a set process to recover any funds due, but you can't do that with a decentralized system which is not owned by anyone.

You might argue that this is one of its disadvantages in that respect, but the reality is that the onus is on the user to keep their keys safe, but also allow for the eventuality of death, for example, by leaving directions to access the wallets in a secure place identified by the will. It's no different to hiding a sum of cash which is impossible to find or leaving a safe deposit key without any identifying marks. In all cases, the money will be lost (in Bitcoin's case it will be stuck forever in a wallet which is visible on the ledger, but not accessible) so it pays to be prepared. Right now, most people are still not considering this enough.

There's one final point to be made about the supply of Bitcoin which is different from other scarce commodities that it is sometimes compared to, the most common of which is gold. Bitcoin has a mathematical certainty of only ever having a maximum of 21,000,000 units (or less in reality as we have already seen), but the actual quantity of gold is unknown in real terms. Its value is based on a perception of rarity, but what if the biggest gold deposits have not yet been located? What if new deposits are found, perhaps deeper down and easily obtainable with new technology, which completely dwarf the existing total supply in the world? What would happen to the price then? Whilst it's unlikely, it's possible, but with Bitcoin, the supply is absolutely finite and can never, ever be altered.

That total is also very important for another reason because it means the currency can never be devalued. Governments are pretty sneaky about printing money when they need a bit more cash for something. Since there's no gold standard and the notes are backed by nothing at all except our belief in them, it's no problem just to run off a few extra million, or billion, when you need it. Of course, this will result in inflation and a lower value of each unit eventually and there's absolutely nothing we consumers can do about it, except vote for a different set of politicians the next time around if it bothers us so much. Politicians, incidentally, who will almost certainly do the exact same thing anyway. Bitcoin's total, on the other hand, can't be touched. Not by the network, not by the consortium of developers who maintain it and not even by Satoshi Nakamoto himself, should he ever re-appear. No-one can devalue your Bitcoin and that provides certainty.

Traders and users of any monetary system like certainty. If we know – completely and utterly – that the supply of an item has an absolute finite limit, then, logically speaking, it is safe to assume there will be a steady increase in price as scarcity kicks in, assuming there is at least some demand for it.

That demand, as we know, is already there because the 'real world' value of it is not zero, so what's causing it and who, exactly, is giving it value? These are great questions and we'll be answering them in the next chapter.

Chapter 8

How Bitcoin has Value - *Part 2*
Demand from 'safe haven' money

"If you guys want proof Bitcoin is real, send them to me. I'll cash them out and feed homeless people."

– Jason King, American philanthropist and entrepreneur

It's all very well creating a really clever decentralized, trustless, secure, self-governing system producing a fixed-supply monetary unit that solves most modern transactional problems, but at the end of the day, if nobody wants it, it's completely useless except as a novelty item.

However, hundreds of millions of dollars globally have now been poured into building better Bitcoin mining machines, more efficient power systems, better networks, new businesses and all manner of related experimental ventures, so someone *somewhere* thinks there's value here at some level. In addition, the daily trading volume of Bitcoin is around $4bn. Yes, that's a BILLION. With a 'B'. It's astonishing, but many think this is only a drop in the ocean for what's coming.

For people like you and me, however, why would we ever consider accepting, using or buying Bitcoin over traditional money such as pounds, dollars or Euros? Incidentally, this 'traditional money' has a specific name in financial circles and its use has grown recently with the growth of cryptocurrency so that it is easier to differentiate between cryptocurrency and traditional currency when discussing the two together. That name is 'fiat' currency and even the origins are strangely relevant to what we're discussing here.

'Fiat' is a Latin word which literally translates as 'Let it be done' and it was used in the context of an authoritarian figure issuing an order. So, for example, a request to build a new marketplace in a Roman town might have received that answer. In the context of money, there is an extra implication – that the money we deal with day to day only has value because the government says it does and for no other reason. That makes sense because otherwise that ten-pound note in your pocket really is only just a posh piece of paper (or, more latterly, a thin and flexible plastic) with some nice pictures on. It only has value for two reasons:

First, because our government has informed us that this is a legal and recognised way of settling debts between people or businesses in our country (but not usually outside of it) and second, because other people are willing to accept it. As mentioned before, it's important to remember that it is not backed by anything at all. Nothing. It has value ONLY because we *think* it does.

When you actually spend some time mulling that over, it's a scary thought. What if, for some reason, we all stopped believing that our pound notes had any value? For example, there might be an economic disaster or the government might be overthrown or our currency was simply deemed not worth buying in the global community. This would lead to a fast drop in value which, in turn, would cause other institutions to cut their losses and dump any sterling they are holding, further depressing the price to an unsustainable level. Those notes would just be pretty pieces of paper and you'd have to find some other way of buying your food, assuming that there was actually any in the shops in that scenario.

As far-fetched as this sounds, it has happened many times in history. And, if you think it only happens in 'third world' countries, think again. In the last two hundred years Austria, China, Germany, Greece, Hungary, Poland, Russia, Turkey, Zimbabwe and (right now) Venezuela have experienced 'hyperinflation' caused by a total collapse in the confidence of their currencies. Many other countries have experienced it too.

All currencies can (and economically speaking SHOULD) devalue slightly over time, the best accepted rate being somewhere around 2%. This is the official inflation figure you hear about regularly on the news at 10 and it's the Bank of England's job to keep it around that level. If it goes too high, say six or seven per cent or even higher, confidence in the currency can start to fall. But if it goes too low, or even negative, it can significantly reduce economic activity to the point where the economy starts to go backward. Two per cent seems to be the magic number.

'Hyperinflation' occurs when the rate of loss of confidence in a currency happens faster than the ability of the mint to produce new notes, although the official definition is more than 50% in a month. For example, no-one will accept a ten-pound note when confidence has fallen so low that the price of a Mars Bar (assuming you could even find one in those circumstances) has risen to £900,000. You'd need 90,000 of them to make the transaction! The sheer weight of all those notes would make it impossible, so the government, usually in a total panic, would simply print £1,000,000 notes instead. Of course, by the time they were available and in general circulation, that Mars Bar might cost £50,000,000. That's a hell of a Mars Bar.

The stories of how people have coped in these countries where this has happened are fascinating. Just after the second world war, Hungary experienced the highest ever rate of hyperinflation, an impossible-to-imagine 42 QUADRILLION per cent. No, that's not a typo, and it's certainly a far cry for the recommended two per cent. In real terms, the value of the currency halved every 15 hours, or, to put it another way, the prices of everything *doubled* every 15 hours. People needed whole stacks of notes bundled together in vast quantities to buy anything at all which created all sorts of logistical problems. One of my favourite stories illustrating the point tells of a lady who used a wheelbarrow to transport an enormous pile of worthless notes to the bakery to buy some bread. Exhausted from the effort, she put the barrow down for a while and walked ahead to the bakery to ensure the bread was actually available. When she returned, the entire pile of money was still there, but the wheelbarrow had been stolen. It was evidently worth more than the money it was carrying.

Whether this story is actually true or just figuratively true remains up for debate, but I have absolutely no doubt that things of this nature really did happen. They're happening right now in Venezuela and it'll happen again in other countries. The American dollar, in particular, is so heavily leveraged and the US deficit is so incredibly large the situation is mathematically unsustainable in the long run. The government will simply be forced to take some action at some point before a critical point is reached. A collapse in a currency as big as the dollar would have devastating effects on the rest of the world and almost certainly bring a few economies down with it. It would all recover eventually of course, but we'd expect the fallout to last many years, certainly decades, and a new form of the dollar would need to be issued.

Whilst this all sounds like doom and gloom, the fact is that it's a natural part of the economic cycle. No currency lasts forever, they just have different lifecycles and once confidence is lost, it can never be recovered and a new currency must be issued in its place. Even the British Pound, recognized as the world's oldest currency at 1,200 years old must, historically and statistically speaking, be replaced at some point.

But what does all this detail and economic history have to do with Bitcoin?

This is all to do with alternatives to fiat money. When currencies have failed in the past, people have been forced to find something else to transact with until the situation is resolved, however long that takes. For day to day transactions that can literally be anything that has a value to most people, and even things like cigarettes and, more recently, mobile phone scratch cards have been used. The point is that it doesn't matter so much what it is, so much as it matters that people will accept it if they know other people will. This, in essence, is no different from the currency it replaced in the first place – it's still about belief and confidence!

But there's another side to it. The traditional safe haven has always been precious metals, usually gold and sometimes silver. Whilst this isn't always available for 'ordinary' folk, it's an historic fact that people who have the means will swap their failing currency for gold, either (and mostly) through direct ownership of the real, physical stuff, or via some form of futures contract or fund, preferably outside of the country that is affected. This increases the demand and since there is a limited supply, the price with it. We see this all the time when there's an economic crisis anywhere in the world. The bigger the crisis, the higher the demand for precious metals and the higher the price.

Suddenly, however, there's a new kid on the block. And this kid is not just for the rich and powerful, he's there for everyone with a smartphone or computer – enter Bitcoin. Now, not only can people swap their failing money for a currency that anyone in the world can accept if they choose to, they can also get their money out of the country that's failing without any risk of it being intercepted or stolen by the corrupt government that usually accompanies (and probably caused) these situations. Whilst Bitcoin has only been around for ten years, and, arguably, only about five years where it's had any real recognition, we've already seen it act as a safe haven in Venezuela and this process is still going on right now.

Inflation rates in the South American country have been as high as 25,000%, so buying, frankly, *anything* that gets your money out of this dying currency is appealing to Venezuelans, but the fact that Bitcoin is so easy to buy for the average person (especially if they are motivated by the economic collapse that is going on around them) makes it an absolute no-brainer. What's more interesting is that even Venezuelans who had bought Bitcoin at the height of the recent – and brief – explosion in Bitcoin price would STILL be better off overall than if they'd left their money in their native Bolivars, and that's after taking into account the decline in the Bitcoin price that followed.

Personally, I suspect that this will happen more and more as Bitcoin becomes more and more well-known, the technology to access it continues to get simpler and easier to use and more and more people accept it directly the same way they would any other fiat currency. Even in countries where hyperinflation isn't happening, but confidence in the underlying currency isn't that high (such as in many African nations), rates of Bitcoin purchase, on average, are higher than most. There were also significant increases in Bitcoin trading volumes from Greece, Ireland, Portugal and Spain in 2015 according to information from some exchanges as the financial crisis continued to bite on those countries.

Whilst this makes sense, this can't be the only reason why the Bitcoin price has risen from just a fraction of a cent to many thousands of dollars, so there must be other factors in play, some of which we'll be finding out in the next chapter.

Chapter 9

How Bitcoin has Value – *Part 3*
Demand from investors

"We have elected to put our money and faith in a mathematical framework that is free of politics and human error."

– **Tyler Winklevoss**, Entrepreneur, Co-founder Winklevoss Capital Management

So, we have a limited supply of Bitcoin which ticks all the boxes for providing something of value and a reason why people who, some would say, have no other choice might buy it, but this is still not even close to being a good reason why you or I might suddenly start using it. With a daily volume of $4bn, there must be other groups of people buying and selling it too, and the most obvious one is investors.

If we knew for sure that Bitcoin was going to be a global currency and everyone was one day going to be using it, then knowing what we know now about total supply and the number of people in the world, it would obviously make sense to buy as much as possible and hold on to it for as long as possible if you wanted to make a substantial profit. At today's prices, roughly $1800 would buy you enough Bitcoin to ensure that you'd own more than 99% of the world's population could ever own, statistically speaking. That $1800 could, in theory, be worth tens or hundreds of times that in just a few short years.

But it's also possible you might be better off taking that $1800 and making a nice fire out of it if the nay-sayers get their way. The problem is, we don't know for sure that Bitcoin will be the global currency that we'd like it to be. Oh, there's not much doubt that a cryptocurrency of some nature will almost certainly be a global powerhouse in, well, probably not that many years, but there's a genuine question over whether it will be Bitcoin. You see, Bitcoin has a few problems.

For all its genius and incredible forethought, there's no denying it's a dinosaur in cryptocurrency terms. It was the first, it was the pioneer and it was the coin that made all others possible, but the fact remains that it is very slow compared to its younger, sleeker, second and third generation counterparts who all took Bitcoin's limitations and built on them. We'll learn more about those guys later, but the point I'm making here is that there is already better technology than Bitcoin out there and some argue that it will knock Bitcoin off the 'top dog' spot at some point. Bitcoin is effectively the reserve currency of the whole cryptocurrency market at the moment but 'first' doesn't always mean 'best'. Just ask Netscape. Or Myspace. Or Nokia. And if you don't know who those guys are, I rest my case.

Because there is an element of doubt, investing in Bitcoin is only for the brave, wise or stupid (depending on who you speak to) but there seem to be a lot of those investors about, probably because there's no denying that it's very, VERY exciting!

You see, like all currencies, Bitcoin's value fluctuates on a constant basis when compared to its 'real world' fiat counterparts like dollars, pounds and sterling. However, whereas the pound may only change a few pennies against the dollar in a day, Bitcoin can vary by literally hundreds of dollars or several percentage points in a day, or even an hour. It's *extremely* volatile, which makes investing exciting, especially when compared to traditional shares which can take years to move. It also makes it extremely dangerous and you need to be careful if you're risking money you can't afford to lose.

Day traders, i.e. those who make very short-term bets on the price of Bitcoin, love it because they can get returns which are totally unheard of in other markets and most of them understand it won't always be this way. As markets mature and more and more users, investors and regulations come in, this volatility will eventually go away, but that's probably some time off yet.

There are other problems with investing in cryptocurrency too, but for many that just makes it *even more* dangerous and exciting! Buying or investing in cryptocurrency is completely and utterly unregulated. That means no protection if things go wrong and, technically, no-one to complain to if you lose your money. This has all happened so fast that governments are really struggling with how to classify it, tax it, treat income from it and even if it's actually legal. Right now, getting involved in the cryptocurrency space is very much taking a trip back to the lawlessness and danger of the old Wild West. Just as was the case then, there are many unscrupulous players looking for a fast buck by preying on people who don't fully understand what they're getting into, and the law is unreliable as no-one is quite sure what the jurisdiction is.

Happily, those days are starting to come to an end, partly as a function of people becoming more educated, but also as systems and technology get better it's harder to fool people. In some countries, governments have already come forward with clear definitions (Canada, Australia, United Kingdom and many others), or legalised it (the previous countries, plus most of Europe, Russia, Brazil, South Africa, Japan, Mongolia, Chile, Iceland, USA, Iraq, Iran and many, many more) and almost all governments are actively looking at how to make it work in terms of tax and how to provide similar protections to consumers, with varying levels of completion. There's no question that regulation is coming though, and that is actually a good thing because it won't be long before Bitcoin will be a properly regulated and protected asset, making it much easier for everyone to use or invest in. Of course, it'll also make it far less exciting, but that's always the trade-off!

Interestingly, only eight countries in the world (as of now) have actually made Bitcoin illegal: Bolivia, Ecuador, Morocco, Algeria, Macedonia, Nepal, Bangladesh and Vietnam. All these countries see Bitcoin as a dangerous competitor to their central currency and are looking to stamp it out before it gets started, with Bangladesh being particularly aggressive to anyone caught trading in it. However, like the internet, it's impossible to stop, and the citizens of these countries continue to use it anyway, they just do it 'off the grid'. I can't help but imagine gangsta-nerds hanging around on street corners whispering "Psssttt, do you wanna buy some Bitcoin?"

With all but eight countries either legalizing or at least 'tolerating' Bitcoin, it's pretty clear that more and more people will start to use it as time goes by. I'm not expecting people like my mum to do this anytime soon of course, but there is a whole swathe of people who are technically competent (that means they can use a smartphone or computer to do, for example, online banking) who are watching and waiting to be convinced either way. As soon as this group joins the party, the Bitcoin price is likely to rocket up. Investors who are brave enough to weather the storm of the anarchy and uncertainty that reigns right now are likely to do very well. But only if they're right, of course.

There is one more thing that is utterly unique about this completely new market that has never happened before in the entire history of global market trading. For the very first time, it is us, the small individual investor, who gets the first bite of the cherry. 'Retail investors' or 'ma and pa investors', as we're better known to 'proper' market traders (y'know, the ones who wear the expensive suits and drive the flashy cars) normally only get the crumbs once the fat cats have been in got their share. Let me explain.

Big financial institutions, fund managers and, in fact, all licensed and regulated financial bodies are not technically allowed to invest in any market that is unregulated. Not a penny. Or they risk losing that precious and very expensive license. They are sitting waiting impatiently for the day they can do so with billions and billions of dollars in investment capital and many, many companies are working round the clock to appease the governmental powers that be to let them in. None have succeeded so far on any grand scale, although there have been a few creative workarounds to date which haven't been massively successful. The pressure on the various national watchdogs or official regulation bodies applied by these organizations has been enormous and this has also encouraged innovation in the sector. Each time they are pushed back with a reason why they're not allowed, they'll go away and work on a solution to that problem so they can apply again, like an excited child who is told they can go to the park when they've done the next chore. Eventually, the child is going to run out of chores and then, well, you'd better be ready to take them.

So, until that happens, you and I have our pick of the currencies we'd like to invest in, including Bitcoin, and we'll only need to pay a low price for it, assuming we're willing to take the risks and deal with any possible charlatans, of course. Once the institutions come and take over the show, we'll either be pushed out or will have to switch to small-scale or long terms gains like we do with stocks and shares. But at least it'll be safer and regulated. You pays your money and you takes your choice (as my old geography teacher used to say for reasons that escape me currently).

For now, then, all the price fluctuations are coming from private investors or ordinary people. It's true that some of these people are very wealthy and, because the market is so small in global terms, they can actually manipulate the price a little through the simple act of trading quantity. This would be totally illegal in any other market, but as it's still not regulated, well, who are you going to complain to? It's like going to an illegal rave with an unlicensed bar and then complaining to the police that you were overcharged for your drinks – you're not going to get much sympathy. That said, you don't want to get caught doing it, because whilst the market is unregulated, the actual act of price manipulation is definitely not allowed, so at least there's a modicum of control in place for what it's worth.

Investing in anything, though, is entirely driven by sentiment. If everyone starts thinking it's the best thing since sliced bread, the price will go through the roof, and as the price goes up, people get scared they'll miss the boat because their mate down the pub 'made a fortune' and buy more, driving up the price further. Known as FOMO buying - it stands for 'Fear of Missing Out' – it's a powerful emotional force that is almost always a bad idea to invest on the basis of. It works the other way too. The slightest drop in price spells panic, people dump their purchases, forcing the price down, which scares other people into selling, forcing the price down further and so on. I mention this because Bitcoin has so far seen at least four full market cycles from one extreme to the other and I have no doubt there will be many more before it finally settles down at some distant date in the future and becomes a proper, 'grown-up' currency.

Until then, it'll be all over the place, but the point is that there are enough investors out there who think this crazy thing will actually work and that makes it very unlikely it will ever fall to zero. And there's one more group of people we haven't even (properly) mentioned yet. We'll cover that next, shall we?

Chapter 10

How Bitcoin has Value – *Part 4*
Demand from users

"Bitcoin will hit thousands of dollars per coin because it's worth at least that much. Or it's worth zero."

– Erik Voorhees, CEO, Shapeshift

So far we've looked at two very distinct groups – people who have no choice but to get out of the situation they find themselves in, such as a collapsing economy, and those who are investing or trading in some way. These two alone have created enough demand for Bitcoin for its price to rise, but there is one more group of people who make the equation work – the people actually using it as a currency.

It's really hard to get numbers on this and different sources cite different ways of coming to their conclusions, but we can safely say that the number of people using it regularly as of today is absolutely tiny, globally speaking of course. Making an educated guess looking at various factors and opinions, I wouldn't be surprised if we were looking at only 20-25 million people worldwide. One recent study put the amount of 'properly' active users at only around 5 million. The point is that while that's definitely a lot of people if you tried to fit them all in one place, it is an almost insignificant number in terms of the 7.5 BILLION people on the planet. However, the number of users is growing daily.

Whilst we can't tell exactly how many people are using it, we can see other statistics that give us a clue. Did you know, for example, that there are Bitcoin cashpoints? You really can go to one of these machines, stick some cash in and get some Bitcoin sent to your wallet on your smartphone, which, for us nerds, is really cool. It's quite telling that there were only about 500 on the entire planet at the start of 2016 and, as of September 2018, there are now 3,661 and growing. There must be a demand *somewhere*, therefore. Of course, these cash points are sometimes viewed with the same scepticism as the original cashpoints were viewed in the late 1960's when they started to appear, but we already know this is normal and will eventually pass. It took about 15 years for that to happen with the traditional ATM, perhaps it'll be the same this time around.

It's possible to see how many 'wallets' people have set up around the world by looking at the 'record sheet' we mentioned earlier and the number comes out to be around 25 million at the moment. There's no limit to the number of wallets you can have and we have to assume a portion are unused, and some people have more than one, so the actual number of users is probably less than this. There are, as we have touched on, lots of other cryptocurrencies which have their own wallets too, but since you normally have to get Bitcoin first to buy them, we can assume that this doesn't mean total additional users.

We can get bogged down in the numbers, but the reality is that whichever way you look at them, we haven't even started yet. There are around $1.5 TRILLION US dollars in circulation right now, which is just one currency accepted in one country, although it is also the international reserve currency. Bitcoin's total market value as of early October 2018 is $114 billion, a mere fraction of just one currency, let alone the total value of the entire planet's physical cash value which is a pretty huge $32 (ish) trillion dollars. So, if you think you're late to the party, you're not. In fact, if you bought Bitcoin now, it would be the equivalent of arriving a week early for the party and demanding dinner and board until it started. Now, THAT'S early.

But there ARE real users. I am one. I have used Bitcoin to buy bits and pieces and I even owned the first café in my hometown to accept Bitcoin at one time. But the reality is, us 'Bitcoiners' are a bunch of people who are happy to put up with the limitations that the system currently has. To use Bitcoin, you need to find someone who will take it in its naked form, i.e., without translating it into fiat money and back again. So, to be precise, someone who is happy to accept 550 Satoshi for a coffee, and then go through a little mobile-phone-and-till-scanning "has it gone through?" dance to get it transferred. At least that's how it used to be. Times, like Bob Dylan said, are a-changin'.

Many of the big moves in the cryptocurrency sphere recently have been about 'adoption', which is basically the word chosen when talking about how many people are using cryptocurrency. The biggest barrier for people wanting to use Bitcoin (after being able to understand it in the first place of course) is that it's still a bit, well, complicated to actually use.

Oh, it would be so easy if we were all geared up to accept multiple currencies in shops, for example. If you could walk into your local WH Smith and pay for your 'Geek Monthly' magazine using any currency you wanted, the systems would probably already be in place, but they're not are they? It's pounds in cash or by plastic, and even the new Apple pay or similar systems are really only a new-fangled way of paying in pounds and making that payment quicker. Accepting Bitcoin requires using a whole separate set up and customer interface, and that's a problem because traditionally they've been a bit slow, fiddly and generally rubbish.

The obvious answer is to use an already established global network and we do have one that's already in place and used by pretty much everyone – the MasterCard and Visa systems. More and more of our payments are being made via plastic (or digital plastic on smartphones) and fewer and fewer by cash. It's easier for us, but also governments like it too for reasons we'll go into later. The trouble is both Visa and MasterCard are run by the banks who, quite obviously, do not want to see Bitcoin - or any other digital currency for that matter – become a mainstream payment system. These organizations stand to lose eye-watering numbers in revenues if that happens so they are not exactly going out of their way to help the situation, even though they may not say it directly.

However, paying by Bitcoin (you can pay using other cryptocurrencies too, but to keep it simple we'll stick with the one we've come to know a bit by now) on the high street is getting easier by the day and there's two 'angles of attack' going on and actually happening right now.

First, there are the high street companies that have geared themselves up to accept Bitcoin in its native form. These guys have installed a more advanced Point of Sale (POS) system that allows them, basically speaking, to switch between pounds and Bitcoin at the touch of a button. Someone wanting to buy something with Bitcoin will usually pay a bit more (the whole system is very young and, as is usual in these situations, prices will fall as adoption grows) and use their smartphone to do it, often by something called a 'QR code' which is that funny looking square-shaped barcode that you often see around on products and adverts. Smartphones scan these and follow a certain instruction or receive some information, such as a Bitcoin wallet address in this case. It's just a simple way of getting to or sending simple information without having to type in something that is usually long and complicated.

Of course, it's not just the system of accepting it that's the problem for these businesses, they need to account for it and pay any taxes as they are legally obliged to. There are some guidelines from HMRC which were created surprisingly early in 2014, but there are still many questions about tax points and values that will only really work out in practice. The fact is that it's so early, there will be some trial and error before it, inevitably, gets as slick as our existing systems are now.

So far, the pattern globally has been that it's only independent shops or small chains that have announced they will accept Bitcoin directly in this way and there are many websites that you can go to that give maps and directions to them, some of which I have listed on my website for you, along with other useful links and resources at www.originalcryptoguy.com, under 'Books by Jason' and the title of this book. I rather suspect, however, that none of these are 100% accurate as they all seem to list different shops in the same location, rather than the same ones, so my advice would be to take it with a pinch of salt and use it as something that's interesting rather than definitive.

The reason for so many independents stepping up over the big stores is most likely logistical since owner-manager operations can easily deal with any 'complicated' transactions personally, although that doesn't always apply. When I owned my retail premises, for example, I trained all the staff to accept Bitcoin as I was only there once or twice a week and the chances are that I wouldn't be there at the right time. The other reason, of course, is the 'leap of faith' required by large organizations managing millions of transactions a day not to mess with the main business and not to create a complex secondary accounting system for something which is, at the moment, still quite small in relative terms.

However, there are a couple of notable exceptions to this. CeX, a national UK chain selling entertainment items such as DVDs, CDs, mobile phones, computer games, consoles and parts has already been accepting Bitcoin both on its website and through its tills for some time now. Some branches of Kentucky Fried Chicken and Subway will also accept it, but otherwise the practice is still not widespread in terms of large, national brands.

Where Bitcoin comes into its own and has a real advantage over traditional systems though, is on the internet. Right back in 1999, Professor Milton Friedman, an American economist who received the 1976 Nobel Memorial Prize in Economic Sciences for his research on consumption analysis, monetary history and theory, and the complexity of stabilization policy (I don't even know what half of that means, but he sounds *really* smart) made this incredibly prophetic statement:

"I think the internet is going to be one of the major forces for reducing the role of government. The one thing that's missing but that will soon be developed is a reliable e-cash."

Remember that was 1999. There was no social media AT ALL. No Uber, no eBay, no iPhone and the internet itself was slow, difficult to use and expensive to access for most people. In reality though, the world only had to wait another ten years before Bitcoin was proposed – that 'reliable e-cash' system had arrived.

This is Bitcoin's native environment. Whilst it can be made to work in the 'real world' (and even that process will soon be as easy as using debit cards as we'll see later) it excels on the internet. This is where code and data is transferred on an enormous and relentless scale every second of every day, so it's a natural move that a portion of it is simply encoded to represent money. But even online, the practice is still not as widespread as you would expect. Although there are a significant minority of companies who have added a 'pay by Bitcoin' button to their checkouts, there are not that many 'big names' in on the game.

However, you might be surprised to discover that Tesla, Microsoft, Dell, Etsy (but only certain sellers), Expedia, Takeaway.com, Overstock.com, Virgin Galactic and Steam all accept, or have accepted, Bitcoin. More are likely to follow as it gets easier and easier to do so and some of the volatility we talked about earlier settles down a bit.

There's also nothing to stop individuals buying or selling things for Bitcoin themselves on big platforms such as eBay and Gumtree and many Bitcoin advocates do this, myself included, just by adding my payment details in like you would for any other system you were using. And it's not just small or second-hand items. Bitcoin has been especially useful for very large money transfers such as for the sale of a house. Yes, not only have lots of people already really done that, but there are, right now, hundreds of properties for sale around the world that can be bought with Bitcoin, although they will usually accept good old-fashioned fiat currency as well. There are even 'Bitcoin only' real estate websites!

All these things, however, are still limited to the people who find it easy to use Bitcoin, despite it still being a bit cumbersome overall. But there have recently been some new developments aimed at bringing Bitcoin, and other currencies, to everyone in a format we all understand – Debit cards. This is the second 'angle of attack' I referred to earlier, and it's arguably the biggest move to date.

Several companies have found a way to work *with* the Visa or MasterCard networks, rather than compete with them. I have, in my wallet (my 'real world' one, the one made of leather than you put on the side when you get home at night), a very normal looking debit card in a particularly fetching turquoise colour issued by a company called Wirex. It acts exactly like a debit card – I can use a PIN or tap it for contactless for items less than £30 – but it doesn't spend the pounds in my bank account - it spends the Bitcoin from my Bitcoin wallet. To be more precise, there's a couple of other types of cryptocurrency I can spend instead of Bitcoin if I prefer, but as we haven't got to those yet, we'll ignore that for now. Given what I said about using Visa and MasterCard networks above, how on earth is this possible?

Before I answer that, I must tell you of a moment that occurred recently that illustrates just how well this bridges the perceived gap between paying with Bitcoin and paying with pound notes. It concerns buying a couple of pints at a bar, something that some of us do quite regularly, and not something you'd generally associate with paying with cryptocurrency.

Last month was my school reunion. It had been 30 years since we'd left as eager teenagers in the summer of 1988. Although I'd stayed in touch with many of the people I'd been at school with, there were a good dozen or so people I hadn't seen for many years. Inevitably, we started talking about what we do and I was pleased to learn that some of my colleagues had done extremely well for themselves and were enjoying a good lifestyle. Equally, they were all completely unsurprised that I was involved in cryptocurrency as I was "always the guy into technology" at school. Not that many of them really knew what it was, but most had at least heard of it.

After visiting the school, having a tour and enjoying a meal back in the main hall, we found ourselves at the pub for a long afternoon session of catching up and having a few too many beers. Whilst crowding around the bar and ordering various rounds, my colleague opened his wallet and I couldn't help but notice a very large wad of twenty pounds notes stuffed, very neatly and all facing the same way, into the last fold.

"Wow, are you expecting a long night tonight!?" I joked in the way you can only do when you've known someone for a very long time and can pretty much say whatever you like.

"Well, you've got to come prepared" he replied, "You can't exactly pay for beers with Bitcoin now can you?"

At that very moment, the barman returned to where we were standing and politely asked for the £18 something he was owed for the drinks I'd bought.

"Oh no?" I said "watch this!" and tapped my Wirex card onto the reader, immediately receiving a satisfying beep.

"That," I said "was Bitcoin."

Of course, the timing of this was incredibly fortuitous and like something out of a film, but life goes like that sometimes. He was intrigued and this led to a more in-depth conversation about how it works and a promise from him that he'll look into it into more detail. He has a very successful business, so I hope he does.

How I did that was actually very simple, and all the credit goes to the company behind the system rather than me as the simple end user. Wirex has simply come up with a clever way of linking fiat money with cryptocurrency. At the point where I tapped the card for my pints of local ale, I was actually spending pounds and pence in the exact same way as I would be if I'd used any of my other debit cards, and, as we know, Visa and MasterCard are happy to provide that service and receive a cut for doing so. The clever bit is the operation that goes on behind the scenes.

My Wirex card is linked to an app on my smartphone and it has a cryptocurrency wallet built in. All I did, before going out in this case (although I could just have easily done it in real time), was transfer some of my Bitcoin over to THAT wallet from the wallet where I normally store it. You can have as many wallets as you like (a bit like bank accounts) and the process of transferring it is really not very different from using any online banking service which most of us are used to these days. That said, given that this book is about explaining this whole thing on a level my mum would understand (she definitely doesn't use internet banking), then it's a bit like transferring cash from one envelope at home marked 'savings' and moving it to one marked 'going out.' Not that she keeps cash that way either you understand, but the visual image of doing that is one that makes sense to everyone.

Once that's done, I can then transfer that into one of the other cryptocurrencies it offers, or simply into pounds and pence at whatever the prevailing rate is, which is what I'd done just before hitting the bar. Genius.

In my view, this is one of the easiest, simplest, most seamless ways there is of using Bitcoin in the real world and this is just the start. There are other cards out there using similar systems and I have no doubt more will come along, but I happen to think Wirex is probably easy enough for everyone to get their heads around, even for people who aren't especially tech or cryptocurrency savvy. The point is that Bitcoin can now be moved, bought and sold in quite large quantities via one simple little app and card, available to anyone and everyone regardless of credit rating, age, status, race, background or existing banking facilities. It'll even work for those who don't have a bank account at all for whatever reason, as they can use cash via a Bitcoin cash machine to buy the cryptocurrency to start with.

And that point alone, for many people, could be a total game changer.

Chapter 11

Is Bitcoin bad for you?

"It's a fraud ... worse than tulip bulbs"

– Jamie Dimon, Chairman and CEO of JPMorgan Chase

For all the great things it promises, Bitcoin has had an enormous amount of negative press, especially in the tabloids. As someone who understands the concept pretty well and is an active user, it can be quite frustrating to see so much incorrect information getting so much attention. Bitcoin (and other cryptocurrencies) seem to be constantly linked to scams, huge losses by individuals and the shady world of crime, presumably because it makes better headlines than something that could solve a lot of the world's problems.

That said, there are definitely some serious problems out there, and being educated about them is will help you navigate the dangers if you choose to get involved at this early stage. In years to come there will be laws, regulations and all sorts of safety nets in place to reduce the likelihood of you losing your money (whether fiat or cryptocurrency), but even so, we have all sorts of regulations and safeguards in the world of 'normal' money we *still* regularly hear stories of people losing their life savings and falling for elaborate scams.

Bitcoin won't solve those problems of course, but it is worth spending some time separating fact from fiction and addressing the comments that seem to come up quite often which seem to be the most pressing issues at the moment.

"It's a scam"

This is probably the most common and normally delivered with absolute, confident certainty by someone who has absolutely no idea what it actually is. Of course it's a scam. That's why institutions want in on it as soon as possible, companies are spending millions developing next-generation systems to work with Bitcoin and other cryptocurrencies and governments across the world are working to try and find a way to make it work with existing systems. Y'know, just like any other scam.

OK, so that paragraph was heavily laden with sarcasm and I also realize the irony of using the very financial institutions who got us into the last global financial crisis as the 'credibility' part of my argument, having already slated them as untrustworthy. However, you'd have to admit, if it IS a scam it's a brilliant one. It's taken ten years, billions of dollars and thousands of people to pull it off so far, and we're still not sure what the 'scam' is actually supposed to be. Also, now that we know that no-one can actually control or manipulate Bitcoin (like a central 'real world' currency can be controlled or manipulated), who exactly is masterminding this and what do they stand to gain?

It's actually more likely, given the evidence, that this is a genuine attempt to solve some of the world's problems and provide an increasingly digital world with a completely digital payment mechanism. It's just meeting with the usual resistance, genuine misunderstanding and suspicion of a 'new thing' that we already know from history is a normal part of the process. True, this jump is probably as big as the jump made by the Chinese merchants back in the tenth century when 'flying cash' suddenly appeared instead of physical coins, but seeing as there aren't any of these merchants around these days, it's kind of hard to ask the question. But I bet you they'd say it's a good comparison. If they could get their heads around it, that is.

"Bitcoin is dangerous. I've heard a lot of people have lost a lot of money"

The second sentence is completely true, but we'll come back to that in a moment. The first point may also be true, but it depends on your point of view.

The original cypherpunks probably would love to think of it as dangerous, anti-establishment, anarchist money, and as we've already seen there's a bit of truth to that. However, Gustav Flaubert (a nineteenth-century French novelist) once observed that "inside every revolutionary is a policeman" which I've always taken to mean that even the most ardent anarchist would agree that anarchy is fine as long as there's some order to it. After all, someone has got to make the petrol that goes in the petrol bombs, right?

If you're a bank, it's a real threat to your existence since Bitcoin is not controlled by a central authority and things like interest rate changes will have precisely zero effect on it. It's entirely possible that children born today will not even need bank accounts since, if cryptocurrency goes the way many expect it to, it'll be a real, viable option worldwide. There are already a few companies offering to pay salaries in cryptocurrencies, there are third-party escrow services for crypto payments and it's even possible to borrow against cryptocurrency assets for mortgages and other purposes. As time goes by, all the traditional financial services offered by banks will be offered via Bitcoin or similar coins. It's happening right now.

Sure, the next generation can have traditional bank accounts as well, but if they're not actually needed, it's a massive threat to your business model. That means reduced lending opportunities, less customer engagement and, ultimately, a lot less profit. You'd definitely classify that as dangerous if you were in that industry.

Governments are also wary and concerned. They really do see it as a danger for a whole host of reasons, the most obvious one being, again, lack of central control, but there's other – quite legitimate – concerns as well. Where will people pay tax? How will it be identified? If it's so easy for people to hide it, how will it be collected? How do you stop people moving money out of the country? Or funding bad guys? We'll touch on some of this later, but if you're in power as a minister or Chancellor of the Exchequer, you'll not be wanting to hand over that control to the people anytime soon.

The other side of this is where people have lost money. That has *definitely* happened and it will happen again as certainly as the sun will rise tomorrow, but this is one you can't pin on Bitcoin itself. This is the nature of investing – you don't always get it right!

You have to remember that when Bitcoin began in early 2009 it had no value at all, it was just a bunch of geeks working on a cool new idea. As it gained momentum, the people who had either mined some Bitcoin themselves or bought hundreds of coins for the spare change they had in their pockets, suddenly found themselves sitting on enormous wealth. Many sold out when the price hit a couple of hundred bucks and then regretted it when the peak of nearly $20,000 was reached in 2017. However, the news was full of people who had become 'overnight' millionaires, or even billionaires, just by holding this weird little Bitcoin thing. The public's attention was peaked and, in what is known in trading terms, the 'dumb money' moved in.

This is quite a rude statement and traders use it to describe 'the herd' i.e., the frenzy that happens when everyone piles in at the same time and tells their mates, who tell their mates and so on and so on. The fact is that the general public is usually not very good at investing in *any* market, let alone something as complex and volatile as the cryptocurrency market. We've seen it dozens of times over many decades in stocks and shares, commodities, tulips, property – you name it, it's happened.

There's a great line in the film 'Men in Black' where Will Smith's character is asking Tommy Lee Jones' character why people can't be told about the aliens living on Earth.

"Why the big secret?" he says "People are smart, they can handle it"

Tommy Lee Jones' character responds "A PERSON is smart. PEOPLE are dumb, panicky, dangerous animals and you know it."

Of course, if you haven't seen this film not much of the context and bit about aliens will make sense, but he IS right in his statement. On our own we're usually capable of working things out and making sensible decisions, but when we're part of a herd, that doesn't always apply and nowhere is this more apparent than in the markets. Bitcoin price goes up like crazy? People react accordingly, moving money from safe haven like savings accounts, selling stuff or, worst of all, borrowing heavily to 'get in on the action'. Eventually, we run out of buyers and the price falls, triggering the exact reverse. The herd panics, sells at a loss to protect what's left of their investment and then complains loudly to everyone about losing money in that 'scam' called Bitcoin. They have just done the exact opposite of what you're supposed to do in a market – they've bought high and sold low, rather than vice versa.

The last point that comes up a lot is the claim that Bitcoin is used only by criminals. This one is interesting because although it's wrong as a statement, there's still a bit of historical truth in there that we need to look at.

We'll need to meet in a remote location to discuss it though and you'll need to come alone.

With cash.

In non-sequential small denominations.

Chapter 12

Bitcoin and Bad Guys

"There are dodgy characters in Bitcoin. But there are dodgy characters in cash too."

– Patrick M Byrne, CEO, Overstock.com

There have always been - and always will be – bad guys, and those bad guys will use every trick in the book to either part you from your cash or find a way to receive a payment for an illegal service without it being possible to track it back to them. Bitcoin, in theory, can help with both of these, hence the association that seems to have evolved. Well, that and the popular press who, rumour has it, likes to sensationalize things to gain sales and increase the value of advertising space. However, the true picture is not quite as straightforward as that.

There are several categories (and scales) of scam, fraud and confidence tricks that currently exist, although they are all pretty much based on the same age-old techniques that have always been around. It's only recently that the bad guys have realized that using Bitcoin as a payment mechanism can be much more efficient. It's all very well accepting payments through credit and debit cards, the *de facto* standard prior to digital currency, but it does mean exposing yourself just a little to the powers that be. That debit card gateway has to be provided by someone somewhere and needs at least some form of very basic ID and a traceable bank account. No, much better to have something completely decentralized and instant, almost 'off grid' in a way. Once you have your Bitcoin, you can sell it easily and almost completely anonymously on an exchange for local currency or simply use a Bitcoin ATM. This means if you can squeeze some Bitcoin out of some unsuspecting mark, you'll be laughing.

For the most part, the scams themselves haven't changed. There are still princes in Nigeria who are sitting on $240 MILLION (TWO HUNDRED AND FORTY MILLION DOLLARS) (they always write the sum in capitals after the numbers don't they!?) which need transferring to you on production of some transfer fees. Your computer has definitely been hacked as the person from 'Microsoft support' who called you randomly says it has, but it can be sorted for a quick payment and a remote control of your machine. Apple Inc. has definitely charged you $300 for an item on your account, but don't worry, you can get it refunded by entering your credit card details and PIN number in the email and sending it back. These scams have been around for years, decades even, in some form or another, the only difference this time around is the payment mechanism that's been gaining in popularity recently – Bitcoin.

One of the big ones at the moment is a new variation of another old classic – the official Inland Revenue notification. These used to be about getting a tax refund for which you'd need to submit your account details (including all the details you'd need to access the account directly, like a PIN number of course) but increasingly this has been about sending official looking emails demanding a tax payment which must be paid immediately in Bitcoin. Now, as unlikely as it sounds that anyone would fall for this, the reality is that the reason these scammers keep doing it is that people DO fall for it - and all the time.

I was contacted recently by a friend of the family who had just discovered that her brother and wife had been handing over huge sums of money to scammers who had posed as tax collectors in Canada. This had been going on for months and every time they paid, another bill was produced, backed with the threat of jail if this wasn't paid over immediately.

What is most astonishing about this case is that neither of the couple were tech-savvy - they didn't even use computers – and they had been contacted by phone. The scammers had patiently talked them through how to withdraw cash and use a Bitcoin ATM, literally staying on the phone as they walked down the street and then talking them through how to load the machine with dollars. The bizarre side effect of this is that these scammers had actually educated someone who had no idea even where to start with Bitcoin into how to use it. But it was an incredibly expensive lesson. They handed over several hundred thousand dollars before the family realized something was going on and stopped it.

The point is that ten years ago, they would have taken credit and debit card numbers using the exact same scam, now it's Bitcoin or other currencies. When it gains acceptance with bad guys in the same way cash has, you know it's a serious contender for a real currency. These guys don't muck about.

We've also seen this with 'ransomware' viruses on PCs. This is where you unwittingly open an attachment on an email which locks down your machine and refuses access until a payment is made to the hijacker. The encryption is impossible to break and the only way to unlock it is to hand over the money. Again, whereas once it was debit cards, now it's Bitcoin. Why? Because it's an incredibly easy, seamless payment system that can't be reversed, exactly like handing over cash face to face. It's perfect for a scammer.

The fact that Bitcoin is so easy as a payment system on a website was not lost on entrepreneurs who operate on the edge of the law either. In February 2011 a 'black market' website called 'Silk Road' (after the ancient trading route) was started by Ross Ulbricht using Bitcoin as a payment method. This site allowed traders, using pseudonyms, to buy and sell anything they want, but really items that were restricted on larger, legitimate sites like eBay. However, Ulbricht argued that the site was not meant to be a haven for the 'dark side of humanity' as it had very specific rules about what was and wasn't allowed to be listed including anything whose purpose was to "harm or defraud". This included stolen credit cards, assassinations and weapons of any type. Which was reassuring. I think.

In reality, the site was used for selling drugs, alcohol, fake driving licences as well as a whole host of legal items such as jewellery, art and cigarettes, and reports that it was actually used for arranging contract killings and the sale of illegal weapons were probably exaggerated. The site was shut down by the FBI in 2013 and a total of 144,000 Bitcoins were seized and later auctioned off. In 2015

Ulbricht went on trial for various charges including those of engaging in a continuing criminal enterprise, narcotics trafficking, money laundering, and computer hacking. He faced 30 years to life if convicted and, in May 2015, (presumably to send a message to other would-be 'libertarians' as Ulbricht called himself) the 31-year-old was given the highest possible sentence; that of life in prison without the possibility of parole. Ever. The Supreme Court also denied him the right to appeal, a possible further indication of how seriously the government took his offence.

Many consider this punishment to be far too harsh for the crime and there is ongoing pressure from several groups to - at the very least - give him the option of parole later in his sentence if nothing else. But whatever your position on this, it did nothing to help the image of Bitcoin and the price went into freefall shortly afterwards due to the sudden dumping of the Bitcoin the FBI had seized on the market and the tarnished reputation Bitcoin suffered in general. It subsequently returned to where it was of course, but the Silk Road story is one that will always be remembered by early Bitcoin enthusiasts, and not too fondly either.

Would it have worked using PayPal or Visa? It's possible, but it seems unlikely given the idea was that total anonymity was the name of the game. In this case, the fact that Bitcoin was accepted was probably a driver for its creation and growth, meaning it's a genuine use case for the dark side of human nature.

Sadly, there have been even more problems with the cryptocurrency industry as a whole, though not necessarily with Bitcoin. Because it's still completely unregulated and everyone is so excited about it (but without really understanding it) all sorts of shady types have crept out of the woodwork to take advantage, usually by creating new bogus companies with flashy websites and ridiculous promises to part would-be investors from their cash. The scary thing is that these have worked really well, and the owners of these sites have absconded with very large sums of money, leaving no trace behind them. Sometimes, as a final insult, they have taken down the flashy website and left only a simple 'up yours' style message on the screen to the dismay of people sitting with empty bank accounts and virtual wallets full of useless coins. The problem got so bad that Twitter, Facebook and Google summarily banned all cryptocurrency ads permanently in early 2018. Unfairly, this adversely affected the legitimate currencies and, a few months later, the ban was all but overturned with some new, strict guidelines in place. What a mess. But also not a surprise.

The same thing always happens the world over when something new comes in and you've got to give these guys some credit for creativity and hard work. I happened to be in Ireland just as the Euro came in at the turn of the century and stories of fake Euro notes were rampant because, of course, most people hadn't seen them yet and had no frame of reference. I'm sure even if I'd printed pictures of the Euros out and written "50 Euro" on them in crayon I'd have had a few takers. Some things will never change.

I should point out that for reasons we haven't yet covered, it's not always (or even usually) Bitcoin that is being used since, as I mentioned before, it's possible to 'see' a version of that big public record we talked about previously. Most baddies, understandably, prefer that not to be the case, even though it's not actually possible to work out who exactly these wallets belong to. Instead, they often prefer other currencies that hide this public record but which aren't – yet – as popular or well known as Bitcoin. We'll be looking at these later but, for now, we'll be just referring to Bitcoin to keep it simple.

What is undeniable though is that the dark side of human nature often leads to the greatest technological breakthroughs. Think of the rocket development by Germany in the latter part of the Second World War designed to kill people that eventually led to the moon landings. Or accelerated nuclear programs to find a way to blast the enemy to small, glowing pieces which were later used to create energy on a massive scale. For a more recent example, take a look at the internet; it was initially a haven of techy people doing techy things with a few interesting early developments going on until someone realised it was a fabulous medium for delivering pornographic content. It's not illegal for the most part, but it definitely falls into the category of 'vice'. This led to better tech to deliver it and faster adoption, leading to the internet we know and love today. Even now, up to 30% of the internet's traffic is still related to pornography. It doesn't look like this is changing anytime soon.

Whilst there's no question Bitcoin has been used for some dodgy dealings in the past, it has almost certainly helped adoption and educated people on how to use it. But the same can be applied to anything, especially the internet itself. Terrorists use social media platforms to extend hate and arrange killings, and drug dealers and money launderers arrange their business through encrypted systems like WhatsApp, but it would be ludicrous (and impossible) to ban the internet because the overall benefits outweigh the negatives. And the baddies would do it anyway. With two cups and a piece of string to make a telephone if they had to. Of course, that would lead to a pressure group banning cups and string and then we'd all be in trouble at water coolers and have to turn to the black market for cardboard coffee cups.

Exact figures are hard to come by, but a fairly detailed search of the net shows that the general view is that less than one per cent of Bitcoin transactions are now related to criminal activities, with 99% being classed as 'legitimate'. The figure was considered to be at least 30% just a few years ago, so this seems to be following the same pattern as we've seen countless times before with new technology. Some sources, incidentally, put the figure at an incredible 90% back in the day, with 10% happening now, but either way, all sources agree that it's a huge drop. Some think that drop will reduce its value as there's less 'users' overall, but as mainstream 'legitimate' adoption takes over any reduction in value is likely to be short-lived. Well, in my view anyway.

In any case, it seems Bitcoin is going straight. And that can only be a good thing.

Especially for my mum, because she worries about that sort of thing.

Chapter 13

Bitcoin and 'The Man'

"Cryptocurrency is such a powerful concept that it can almost overturn governments"

– Charles Lee, creator of 'Litecoin'

This one is interesting for reasons we have already touched on. The bottom line is that governments really don't like Bitcoin or any of the other currencies very much at all and they would prefer it all went away for good.

In reality, I think there's also a bit of sour grapes about the whole thing because if THEY had thought of it and issued their own cryptocurrency, it would all be fine and we'd now be using a digital version of pounds, dollars and Euros instead. It's not an unreasonable idea, but you're still stuck with the same problem of the valuation being in someone else's hands, an almost certain central control (they'd never relinquish this and you'd have to trust it) and the sticky issue of how to move the money across borders. There's never a complete answer is there?

One country has actually tried to issue a national cryptocurrency already and that story is unfolding even as I type these words. The 'Petro' is a new cryptocurrency issued by the very country we were discussing previously in terms of hyperinflation – Venezuela. It's allegedly backed by real oil and mineral reserves and, in reality, is probably no more than a blatant attempt by a corrupt government to prop up its failing currency, buy favour with the international community and get round the US sanctions it still has imposed on it. Many doubt that the oil and mineral reserves it is supposed to represent even exist and no real auditable data is available about the whole thing. It represents, at the very least, an incredibly risky investment and, in my view, will almost certainly fail.

Quite conveniently for my purposes, we can all point to it and say "see, that's what happens when you let a government get involved" although, in the interests of balance, we'd also have to point out that this is one of the worst possible governments you'd ever use as an example of something like this. It's a bit like putting the school bully in charge and asking them to look after the little kids while the teacher is away. It isn't going to end well and no one is going to be surprised by that, only by the fact that somehow someone thought it was a good idea in the first place.

Most people would agree that having Bitcoin completely decentralized and self-governed is the safest way to go, particularly when you consider our collective history of dealing with money and each other. It's why we, as people collectively, can't have nice things. We simply can't be trusted with them. But, as usual, solving one problem creates a whole bunch of other ones.

In terms of Bitcoin, it threatens to reverse something the government has been working on for decades, that is, the ability to track money, specifically where it's going to and why. There are all sorts of legitimate reasons for this of course; we really don't want to be funding terrorists, or allowing criminals buy and sell weapons or drugs or allow rogue states access to funding, but how far is too far? How much freedom do we need to sacrifice to keep us safe? Many people already think it is way, way too much.

The fascinating truth is that we've really only been able to do this – properly anyway - for less than one generation. Prior to this the technology just wasn't good enough, or at least not good enough to do it in real time. We have, on a daily basis at our fingertips, access to better technology now than the secret services had twenty years ago. There is more computing power in your phone than was on the entire planet only fifty years ago and even my mum's phone has more computing power than NASA had when they sent men to the moon. Probably only just though. It really is very, very old.

So, if we've only been able to do this for a generation, how did we survive before that? For the previous several thousand years, that is. Well, we did. Oh, this isn't a 'harken for the old days' lament - almost everything is much better than it was - but we had a much higher degree of freedom on everything than we do now, with all the good and bad things that brings. The government still had a fair idea of what we were up to, but not quite to the same degree, and being a criminal was both easier (fewer checks and fewer monitoring systems) and harder (poorer comms, trickier co-ordination). Like all arms wars, as one side developed a better armour, the other side developed a better bullet, but in the end most of the casualties were civilian and resulted in the losses of certain liberties. And yet we had survived for years, decades, centuries and millennia before the hardcore monitoring systems came into place.

This has all got unintentionally rather political, but the point is Bitcoin reintroduces a freedom that was being slowly removed through legislation and the installation of systems 'for our own protection.' Viewed from that angle, it's potentially a BIG problem for governments. You can see how it would be easier for them if it went away and never came back.

The other part of this is cash, that is, physical notes and coins in your pocket. Although these are entirely official and issued by our governments, those same governments are trying to wean us off it. It simply isn't traceable if money passes between us and we don't tell anyone. That can also be a problem 'The Man' doesn't like. Let me demonstrate.

Imagine you're the Chancellor of the Exchequer for the moment. Now, imagine that every single transaction is done ONLY via electronic means. There's no cash used anywhere at all for anything and notes and coins are now curious collector's pieces with no value at all, the sort of thing that grandparents drag out of little cardboard boxes and show bemused children with long, complicated explanations of what it was used for. You, as Chancellor, can now account for every penny of the issued money stock in real time. You can see who is buying what and where money is going. You'll be able to collect all the taxes due because there are no 'cash' jobs and everybody's true income and expenditure is apparent. What a great position it would be in both from a political and security point of view. It's where, ultimately, all governments would like to be and many have been quietly working towards this for some time.

But it's not so great from a citizen's point of view though, is it? That information will obviously be leaked or sold, the security will be misused and the data will be used for less than reputable purposes as it always *always* is. You're back to the problem of putting all the power in a few people's hands again, whatever the government structure you're living under. However, if you look at what has been going on for the last few years, we've been edging closer to that position.

Cash is falling out of favour. It has become possible just in the last few years to live entirely without it, using only cards or smartphones to pay bills online, in shops, for taxis, even borrowing a tenner from your mates down the pub. There are now no minimums for credit card spend, no charges for the customer and contactless technology means it's even easier to pay for anything, instantly and painlessly. All at the cost of being traceable, and that works perfectly for the powers that be. Derek "Del Boy" Trotter, on the other hand, is not best pleased.

Bitcoin, again, threatens all that. It's modern, especially compared to old-fashioned cash, and has all the advantages we've already touched on, especially the ones that allow complete freedom of movement and allow anybody, even people right at the bottom end of the wealth scale who would never be allowed a bank account, to transact on an equal playing field with anyone else. It's also, in the traditional sense, not traceable and it's constantly changing value is a challenge for organisations. While the government has been striving and working hard for the day we all spend 'on the books', Bitcoin has effectively come along and has the real potential to completely derail that project. We can now buy our

'New Socialist' magazine for a few Satoshi without 'The Man' ever knowing. So there.

Of course, as I type this and re-read what I've written, I realise I sound a bit like an angry, 20-year-old, left wing 'smash the state' student version of myself, rather than the middle class slightly conservative person I am supposed to be at the age and position I am in now. However, I am the first to admit that a country entirely and solely run on Bitcoin is an economist's nightmare for all sorts of reasons I don't plan to go into here. One is unlikely to exist without the other now that the genie is out of the bottle, and the two – Bitcoin and fiat currency - have to co-exist somehow. They have to be able to tolerate each other, like a disgruntled divorced couple putting the kids first and agreeing to compromise on a few things.

How would this work exactly? Well, I hope you weren't reading this book for an answer to that because I don't have one and I don't think anyone else does yet either. But I do know we need to be working on it. We still need to have taxes paid. We still need to ensure that bad guys don't get funding for their projects and we still need to ensure that there is some monetary control at a local level because economies need to do be able to do that. But there should be total freedom for individuals to use and spend their money how they wish to do so, without being forced to use an 'inferior' system (which is how many Bitcoiners now see it) because governments say they have to. History tells us this never ends well for the governments who try to force their people to do anything against their will.

We've been here before, of course. There was tremendous concern about the internet when it first evolved, especially about how it could seriously jeopardise trade, circumvent sanctions, allow better communication for terrorists and make tax avoidance easier. This all sounds uncannily familiar to where we are now and, after a lot of trial and error and learning from each other, most of the day to day issues concerning the internet are resolved. We're still finding new issues all the time, but we'll deal with all of those as we go because the internet is here to stay and is a key part of everyone's lives. My personal view is that Bitcoin will go the same way.

Banks are even more fearful of this due to the potential loss of power and profits they would face if Bitcoin ever did go mainstream. The profits made by banks are gigantic, routinely reporting quarterly profits of $5bn a quarter, or $20bn a year. To work out what that was on an hourly basis, I was dismayed to see that my calculator didn't even have enough noughts available – THAT's how big the number is. (If you're interested, it's $2,283,105 each and every hour, even while you're sleeping, and that's PER BANK, not all of them combined!)

That sort of money is enough to make anyone protective, so the banking system has been openly, but subtly, making life just that little bit harder for people trying to use Bitcoin. Many banks banned people from buying cryptocurrency via their credit cards, citing 'consumer protection'. Some mortgage lenders refused to lend money on properties where the deposit had been gained through cryptocurrency and many companies dealing in cryptocurrencies in any shape or form in the UK have found that their banks will not supply them with any facilities, forcing them to move overseas. Banks, like governments, are a bit miffed about the fact that they didn't think of it first.

Banks have since decided they want to develop their own cryptocurrencies in some cases, but they will have all the same problems that the government-backed schemes would have that we identified at the start of this chapter. It might be even worse this way round because these cryptocurrencies would be in the hands of people who caused the credit crunch. By fraud. And ultimately were not held accountable in any real terms. Doesn't sound quite so good when you put it that way, does it?

My mum, of course, won't be concerned with all of this, but she *is* concerned that all the banks in the village where she lives have now closed down, even though we used to have four when I was growing up in a place that had half the population it does now. It's a sign of the times that the banks themselves have pushed through the closures as they claim we can do everything digitally now - online banking, smartphones, automated phone systems etc. – but not *too* digitally of course, i.e., using Bitcoin. It also helps keep those profit margins growing as a high street presence is expensive. That said, my mum still blames me for all the shops closing down because of online shopping. It was, apparently, all due my time at 'Microwave' doing some 'advertising or something'. She doesn't seem to be blaming me for the banks, though, and for that I'm grateful. It may, however, only be a matter of time.

Wherever you stand on the freedom vs security debate, make no mistake that Bitcoin is not popular with governments, central banks and traditional commercial banks as these institutions have the most to lose with every step forward that Bitcoin makes. Governments are notoriously useless at working together, so a global agreement on regulation and approach, even if it were possible, would take years, by which time Bitcoin, or something very similar, may well already be a mainstream currency. Even if just one country allows transactions to be completed in it (and many countries have already stated they are 'pro' Bitcoin) the global nature of the system means that the entire planet can still transact in it, no matter what its neighbours say or try to do to stop it.

No-one knows the answers or exactly what problems will really arise, but one thing is for sure: the world of finance is about to change forever.
Indeed, it already has.

Chapter 14

So, will Bitcoin work or not?

"I do think Bitcoin is the first [encrypted money] that has the potential to do something like change the world."

– **Peter Thiel**, Co-Founder of Paypal

Bitcoin is incredibly divisive. There are just as many leading strategists and business people who have come out in gushing support of Bitcoin (or at least cryptocurrency in general) as there are who are vehemently against it, calling it a 'scam', 'Ponzi scheme' or simply 'worthless.' If we put all these people in one room it would get very, very messy. But if the world's leading economic and business brains can't even agree, what hope do WE have?

Well, I have my own answer to that. These folk try and predict the future based on economic and business trends, their own experience and education and how they see people interacting on a global scale. These are extremely hard things to try and predict with an enormous number of variables, so it's easy to see why you could come up with a rational argument one way or another and support it with pretty convincing evidence. You also have to take into account what their agenda is.

It would be so easy if all the business people were 'pro' Bitcoin and all the banks and governments were 'anti' Bitcoin as this would very neatly support all the points I have made so far and keep the conspiracy theorists happy at the same time. The problem is that this isn't true. Bitcoin has support – and opposition – from each of the areas, and some of them are quite surprising because they are the polar opposite of what you might expect.

Bill Gates, arguably one of the last century's greatest businessmen (and my old boss), seems to be against Bitcoin at the moment, although some of his earlier quotes were generally supportive. Early in 2018 on CNBC's Squawk Box, he called it a 'greater fool theory' investment, later adding that 'he'd short it if he could'.

'Shorting' is an investment term for betting on the price of something falling rather than rising. Strangely, Bitcoin is really quite easy to 'short' as many people have pointed out to Bill, but as far as we know he hadn't taken them up on the offer so far. 'Greater fool theory' is the idea that something only has value because someone more stupid than you is prepared to pay you more than you paid for it, and so on. In short, Bill definitely wasn't being kind here.

But Richard Branson, someone who could also claim (if he ever wanted to) the same 'greatest businessman' title, is entirely PRO Bitcoin, describing it as "driving a revolution". I have been fortunate enough to meet both of these business leaders over the years and they both have a natural presence, confidence and authority about them that makes you want to listen to their point of view. How, though, do you reconcile these completely opposing views from two very similar mindsets?

If leading businessmen can't agree (and there are many more on both sides of the argument), what about large-scale investors? Here too, the story is not clear-cut. The most famous investor of the modern day would probably be Warren Buffet, and he is on record as being, well, really quite rude about Bitcoin, recently going as far as saying that it is 'rat poison squared'. It's an odd statement, but I think the message behind it is clear.

Other large-scale investors such as the Winklevoss Twins (of Facebook fame) have the polar opposite view claiming Bitcoin will reach "40 times its current value" in the future. They are a real tour de force in pushing for recognition of Bitcoin by the SEC (Securities and Exchange Commission) in the USA so that institutions can invest directly into it and start using it. Many people, including myself, think they could succeed as soon as 2019.

Economists are the only group who aren't quite as divided, with the majority coming out against Bitcoin citing traditional macroeconomic arguments. Just recently, 'Dr Doom' the economist who correctly forecasted the economic crash in 2008 (also known by his real name of Dr. Nouriel Roubini) has been an outspoken critic of Bitcoin. He seems actually furious about it - there's simply no other way to describe his vitriol. In October 2018, he was asked to present his thoughts to the United States Senate Committee on Banking, Housing, and Urban Affairs concerning Bitcoin. His tirade was full of four letter words and extreme hatred for the whole idea of cryptocurrency. He is keen for it to fail. He's not the only one.

There are many other economists who share his view, most notably Nobel Prize winner Joseph Stiglitz and his fellow Noble Laureate Paul Krugman. Both are extremely critical and cynical about Bitcoin and whether it will ever have any 'real' underlying value. The few economists who have anything good to say about Bitcoin seem to imply that the old economic tests that their colleagues are applying are outdated and can't apply in this case because it's a whole new concept with no real precedent. It's an enormously complex area, and only time will really tell.

Even with governments we find differences as we have already seen. Countries such as Malta have stated publicly they are 'cryptocurrency friendly' largely due to the almost fanatical support of its Prime Minister Joseph Muscat. Malta is proactively positioning itself to attract as many new generation businesses to the island as possible with the aim of creating the global cryptocurrency centre of the future. Other countries have made it clear that it isn't welcome, going to extreme lengths (usually unsuccessfully) to make sure their citizens can't use it.

With so many smart people having completely opposite views it makes coming to a conclusion about the future of Bitcoin extremely difficult for the average person in the street. It gets even more complicated when you look into the backgrounds of the people involved.

Many of these people are well known in their fields because they have 'got it right' enough times to be remembered for it. But they've all got it wrong as well.

Both Bill Gates and Richard Branson have made the wrong call and have several business failures to their name, like any other businessman.

Investors rarely get every investment right. Warren Buffet has lost millions in poor investment decisions, often citing Tesco's, Dexter Shoe Co and General Reinsurance as the ones he shouldn't have invested in and Google and Amazon as the ones he should have when he had the chance to do so.

Dr Doom has been consistently predicting another market crash every year since 2012 but, in fact, it has just been through six years of enormous growth. It will crash again, ultimately, so will he claim is he is 'right again' then? Noble winning economist Paul Krugman confidently predicted in 1998 that the impact the internet would have on the world's economy would be no better "than a fax machine's" and that everyone would realize this by 2005 because people "have nothing to say to each other". This man won a Nobel Prize. He's *incredibly* smart and yet could not see the internet for what it would become. It seems astonishingly sort sighted in retrospect.

The thing is, although it's reassuring for us mere mortals that these incredibly smart, world-leading thinkers get it wrong as much as we do whichever side of the Bitcoin argument they're on, I'm not sure that helps us any. Sure, we can listen to their point of view and arguments, but the fact is that this is potentially more revolutionary than the invention of the internet and is probably the biggest financial change the world has ever faced. There's no precedent. We're going to have to make it up as we go.
And I find that terribly exciting.

Chapter 15
Why Bitcoin *will* work

"I think the fact that within the Bitcoin universe an algorithm replaces the functions of the government … is actually pretty cool. I am a big fan of Bitcoin"

– Al Gore, 45th Vice President of the United States

I make no secret of the fact that I am pro-Bitcoin and later on I'll share why I am so passionate about it and what good I believe it can do for the planet. Those of us who believe that Bitcoin will work and ultimately be a real, global currency understand that to get to that point a whole lot of things would need to happen first and probably in a certain order. In this chapter, we'll have a look at those things and assess how likely they are to come to pass. In the next, we'll look at why it may never happen and the reasons the doomsayers might be right. You'll then be able to a make your own assessment about where we go from here. Well, as much as any of us can anyway. Predicting the future is tricky and, as we've already seen, even the 'experts' can't even agree.

The most important point for me is simply the concept that Bitcoin is an idea whose time has come. This really could not have worked at any previous time in human history. First, because the technology wasn't there and second, there was no real reason not to trust the banking system. A combination of these two things coming together at the same time at a particular point in history has created a unique situation that could allow Bitcoin to thrive and gain a position of unassailable dominance. Sometimes, like the creation of life itself, the conditions just need to be exactly right.

I don't think it's a coincidence that various studies conducted by Facebook Research and major technology conglomerates have shown a clear trend of millennials shifting from legacy banking systems to innovative alternatives such as a new generation of financial applications. This is no doubt due to both of the reasons mentioned above – technology and trust. This generation is also the first growing up in a truly digital world where apps for everything are the norm and for them, this is a completely natural step. For us older lot, who had to rely on physical visits to the library to find stuff out or queue up in a bank at lunchtime with a chequebook, it's not quite as straightforward, but we'll get there. We managed to work our phones, didn't we? Well, mostly. And only when we have our reading glasses.

The new generation is now used to making instant payments online at any store either directly on a virtual checkout or by using PayPal, paying their mates or bills via Paym or Pingit or paying for taxis instantly and automatically via an app when using Uber. This generation more than any other can't therefore understand why it takes so many days and costs so much to send money abroad or between banks. Three to five working *days*? How is that even a 'thing?' It just doesn't make sense to them. The problem is that our banking system has not moved with the times and the task of changing it is expensive, incredibly slow and, until recently, there was a complete lack of will to make it happen. The reality is that now they will probably not make it in time before cryptocurrency becomes a real, viable alternative.

It's not fair to say, however, that most Bitcoin users are generation Z (that's people born after around 1995), because it's simply not true. That said, I must admit I'd had the same thought until I attended The Crypto Investor Show at the QEII Centre in London in early 2018. The show was completely packed having sold out previously - which was a surprise to me in itself - but the other thing that struck me was that not only were both sexes represented equally, but the number of different backgrounds, ages, races and colours looked like something from a BBC production diversity inclusion checklist. It was great to see and re-assured me once again that Bitcoin has universal appeal.

Generally speaking, people who hold Bitcoin are also quite passionate about why they're holding it. For some, it's just the fact that they may make some money on it one day, but for many others it is what it represents – the future. And, of course, passionate people make great advocates and evangelists, constantly introducing Bitcoin to new people spreading the virus further and further. But something else happens too, because everyone who owns Bitcoin also becomes a stakeholder in its success. In other words, the more people who hold or use Bitcoin, the more people want it to succeed. The more people want it to succeed, the more desirable and valuable it becomes. The more desirable and valuable it becomes, the more the price rises relative to supply. As soon as the price rises, the herd piles in and wants some of the action and the dance goes on, probably in boom and bust cycles (Bitcoin has already seen at least four of those!) but always on a generally higher trajectory. At some point, the snowball effect will happen. If you're a Bitcoin believer that is.

Personally, I think enough money, expertise and belief is already 'in the system' to make it unstoppable from this point going forward. Yes, it's *incredibly* early days with only a few million active users, but the fact that these few users have created such a stir and created so much global attention in such a relatively short space of time must, surely, be an indicator of the future. If just 1% of the world's population adopts it in the next few years – something that seems completely inevitable at this stage – it will create a user base three times what it is today. That will bring three times the activity, daily volume and, most likely, price. If that happens, you can be sure that getting to 2% of the global population will take far less time than it took to get to the first 1%.

This has not escaped the attention of the big financial institutions, almost all of whom are investing enormous sums of money preparing themselves for the day they will be allowed to invest on behalf of their clients. The sheer size of the dollar amounts being thrown about are mind-blowing and if (and it really is an 'IF' at the moment) they are given the green light to go ahead, the effects are likely to be instant, enormous and permanent. Bitcoin's global market capitalisation (that is the amount of Bitcoin in existence times the current market price) is only about $114bn globally. This is tiny. This is less than is traded in gold – just one commodity amongst thousands – per *day*. It's so small it's almost insignificant to these investors, but the very act of them getting involved will change all that immediately. It would be quite the ride, especially if you were holding any Bitcoin yourself at that point.

By reverse engineering the logic here, the only way you would NOT therefore invest in Bitcoin is if you were absolutely 100% certain it will fail. Now, many of the diehard anti-Bitcoin naysayers would happily subscribe to that position, but I bet you that even some of the people who only think it 'probably' won't work will grab a few Satoshi anyway 'just in case'. The very act of doing so, of course, drives up the level of scarcity and you've just reinforced what it is you were campaigning against. It will be fascinating to see who eventually comes out as holding what.

As compelling as all of this is, these are really only interesting distractions. The real value of Bitcoin lays in its design and what it was created for. The bottom line is that the world is ready for, and needs, a simple global payment system to work in a global marketplace. Many think it won't actually be Bitcoin itself as it has some speed limitations compared to its newer counterparts so one of those may well take that spot in time, but there's little doubt in these circles that Bitcoin itself, being so massively supported via its network globally, will remain for good. BUT, it may well fill slightly different roles – first as a digital version of gold (a 'store of value') and, second, as the reserve currency of cryptocurrencies, a bit like the dollar is today in the physical world.

Gold has had a great run but, as we've seen already, it's not that easy to work with for most people. You have to know what you're doing and you have to know the right people. I'm not saying it's impossible, but it's not as straightforward as you might think and you can't just walk into a high street store and buy it. Well, unless you want it in necklace or ring format, but that's not quite the same thing. Bitcoin, though, is immediately available to anyone with basic technical knowledge in any quantity according to the budget they want to set. It's an obvious improvement for so many reasons and many people, including myself, see it as a natural route for Bitcoin to take, although it's very unlikely it would actually replace gold in its entirety.

The best way to think of it is like the difference between your current account and your savings account. In the former, your paycheque comes in and you pay your bills, buy your food and you might save a little. You'd use this account to pay for your coffee on the way to work in the morning because it's quick, easy and instant.

No-one, on the other hand, uses their savings account to buy a coffee and that's ok because it's not designed to do that and it would be awkward to do in practice. The idea of a savings account is that you put your money aside so that it's not necessarily easily accessible in return for some interest. This is a fairly close analogy for Bitcoin – it's basically your savings account. If economic theory is correct and adoption happens, then the value should continue to steadily increase over time (as it has done consistently so far, despite the day to day volatility) and you'd use it only for large purchases, such as a house or car. It's not completely accurate though because it's still easy to get to your money, it's just that it's not fast enough to use for day to day small transactions. It takes time for the network to process and confirm everything, sometimes up to an hour, whereas a debit card transaction takes seconds. Using Bitcoin, your coffee would be cold by the time you were able to leave the store.

That said, there's a large group of very clever people working on a solution called the 'Lightning network' which is designed to solve that problem for good, but it's too early to say if they're going to be successful. If they are, this will remove the main limitation of Bitcoin overnight and it will be a game changer from that day on. Cars, houses, coffees, packs of gum – it would all be possible, and instant, with Bitcoin.

But even assuming that the Lightning Network is not successful for some reason, when the day comes to buy your house with Bitcoin, it's also very cheap to move that money about. Recently, one of the largest ever Bitcoin transactions was carried out by a private user where 29,999 Bitcoins were moved from one place to another. The value of these coins was about $194m at the time and the cost to do this through the traditional banking sector would have been in the tens of thousands of dollars. With Bitcoin, the total fee was 10 cents. It's unlikely that traditional banking would ever be able to match that, but this one transaction neatly shows why people are so excited about the possibilities that lay ahead. And why the banks don't want it to happen.

Of course, it's still all early days and the technology is advancing as fast as we're learning and adapting in the same way that mobile phones and the internet did. Moving money between fiat and cryptocurrency is still a bit of a faff, and sometimes expensive, but that is changing all the time. There is one aspect of this that could still secure the future of Bitcoin permanently – Bitcoin has become the de facto reserve currency of the entire cryptocurrency world.

You see, when you convert your fiat money into cryptocurrency, you usually have to buy Bitcoin first. Of course, once you'd done that, you can instantly transfer it between any currency that takes your fancy for a small fee, like you would dollars to pesos or euros or pounds. Turning it back into fiat requires going through Bitcoin again, making it the gateway of all transactions. Now, this may change in the future, but it is now likely that Bitcoin is so entrenched into the system that it will always be the standard that it is measured against. Indeed, many traders measure other currencies in Satoshi rather than pounds and pence or dollars and cents and it's hard to see that changing at the moment. It's not impossible of course, but the balance of probabilities makes it less likely. That being the case, Bitcoin is positioned to remain the 'gold standard' of the cryptocurrency world for some time yet, possibly forever.

Apart from the enormous security of the technology that we've already looked at (and don't need to revisit again you'll be relieved to know) there is one more aspect of Bitcoin that makes it likely that it will survive in the long term; it is incredibly - even astonishingly - resilient. Bitcoin simply seems to be able to survive anything thrown at it and then come back even more powerful than before.

This has not been lost on Ofir Beigel, the creator of the website 99Bitcoins.com, who has created a now famous 'obituary page' listing every time Bitcoin has been formally denounced, debunked, 'exposed as a scam' or simply declared dead by the media. At the last count, Bitcoin had received 314 funerals spanning eight years. Some of these articles, even from leading publications such as Forbes, CNBC and The Economist, claimed as far back as 2011 that the 'game was over' for Bitcoin and it would never survive. For each entry, the full article is included and, presumably as a slightly smug reminder to the naysayers, the price of Bitcoin at the time is emblazoned next to it. Even at 23 CENTS a Bitcoin it was apparently doomed to fail. It's currently sitting at $6700 and still having to deal with the exact same press.

To be fair to the commentators, we saw the same thing with the internet and certain tech stocks, especially Amazon who seemed to be constantly vilified in the press for its business model. It's part of forging a new path, a sort of rite of passage and, if history tells us anything, almost certainly means we're on the right track.

But that doesn't necessarily mean it will work. There's a lot of people who really want to see Bitcoin and its fellow cryptocurrencies fail for lots of different reasons, so we need to understand their point of view too. Let's have a look.

Chapter 16

Why Bitcoin *won't* work

"Bitcoin has pretty much failed thus far on the traditional aspects of money. It is not a store of value because it is all over the map. Nobody uses it as a medium of exchange."

– **Mark Carney,** Governor, Bank of England

Bitcoin, as much as we'd love it to be, is not a Utopian solution to everything. The technology is groundbreaking, the theory is fantastic, but the execution is not as good as we'd like it to be.

Bitcoin's tech uses something called the 'Blockchain' which is a word you have probably heard being thrown about loosely in the press and in conversations about it on the telly. I have deliberately avoided using this word until now as it starts to head back into technical detail, but remember that 'big record of everyone's transactions' I was talking about some chapters ago? That's basically the Blockchain. It's a long chain of information that is added to every time someone moves Bitcoin about and is the thing that makes it impossible to forge or cheat. The blockchain is the underlying breakthrough technology that makes all of this work as it should. It has many other applications through lots of other areas of life which are being explored now by a whole new generation of companies, but that's beyond the scope of this book.

In the ideal world, the blockchain should be secure, scalable (i.e. can easily be increased in size without affecting performance) and decentralized (i.e. not controlled by one person or a small group). The truth, however, is that no-one has yet found a way of making a blockchain work with all three of these components working smoothly at the same time. You can have any two you like, e.g., secure but centralised OR scalable but not secure, and in Bitcoin's case, it is secure and decentralised but it is not, technically, scalable. This is a problem and we have already seen an instance of that in the recent craziness when huge daily volumes of Bitcoin were traded in December 2017 and January 2018.

At that time, everyone went Bitcoin crazy. Money poured in from all angles and everybody and their dog wanted some. The network that supports Bitcoin became overloaded. This meant that transactions between wallets were backing up and the only way to 'jump the queue' and get your Bitcoin transferred was to 'bribe' the miners to move yours first. It's not really supposed to be a bribe, it's actually a nominal fee automatically added to all transactions to compensate the miners for their equipment and power and, as we've seen, this is usually pretty small, in the region of a couple of cents. However, it effectively became a bribe as people started bumping up their offers to get theirs moved first and, as you might expect, it got completely out of hand.

The best way to describe this is to imagine a bus stop in a village. There's a bus to town every two hours with 50 seats available and anyone who wants to can get on it and pay a few pence to the driver to compensate for his time. Usually, there are quite a few seats spare and the whole thing runs easily and smoothly. One day, however, 60 people turn up wanting to get on the bus and some of these people don't want to wait for the next one. So they have a quiet word with the driver and offer a higher fare than they normally would, allowing themselves priority over the people who can't, or won't, pay. The ones left over wait for the next bus and no doubt have a good moan about it while they do so.

However, there's now already ten extra people at the bus stop and this time 100 new people turn up, all expecting to get to town for their meetings and appointments. The first ten, who didn't want to pay two hours previously, now realise they are going to have to up their game if they're going to get on. This time the fares are even higher as there are even more people, and since there's going to be more people left over for the next bus, the process will accelerate again. Meanwhile, the driver, who has realised what is going on, is having a great time and keeps increasing his minimum demands as far as he possibly can to take advantage of the situation and so it continues until the demand starts to fall back to normal levels and prices.

This is exactly what happened at the turn of 2017, except using our village bus example it was thousands rather hundreds of people who turned up. Prices absolutely skyrocketed and one of the big advantages of using Bitcoin - how cheap it is to move around - was temporarily lost. This is exactly what the Lightning Network is trying to resolve, but it's not easy as you can't just change the underlying technology for reasons we've already discussed. The only way to do that would be to create a whole new currency with better, more efficient processes and start again. This is effectively what some of the new currencies I've mentioned previously have done, so instead of one bus every two hours, there might be one every hour, or even every 5 minutes and they'd be much larger, but the concept is exactly the same. The Lightning Network is working to solve the problem but they can't increase the bus size or the frequency they come at as this is locked into the code that Bitcoin runs, so you can imagine how tricky that would be! The boffins behind it have already created a structure that will, in theory, work, but it's still in testing and could be years before it becomes a standard. Who knows where Bitcoin will be then? Will it be too late?

The next problem is the underlying value. People who are against Bitcoin often cite the fact that it has nothing to support it, i.e., there's no underlying value or 'gold standard'. We've already discussed this at some length and my firm view is that if Bitcoin fails it is almost certainly NOT going to be for this reason. In my opinion this has all but been disproved because we already know that no 'real world' currencies have any actual backing either and people will trade with anything that they believe has value whatever a government or any other central body says about it. Bitcoin clearly has *some* value since it never trades at zero, although I would agree it's hard to decide what that actually is. At the end of the day, the markets will decide that, but for reasons of inclusivity it had to be repeated here.

Bitcoin's biggest strength is also one of its biggest weaknesses – the fact that its technology and actual concept is hard to understand at first. It's probably even why you bought this book. It is SO different to anything we're used to, we all really struggle to work out how to use it and how it fits in with the real world. Add into the mix that we have a natural tendency to be extremely suspicious about 'new money' and most of us will tend to dismiss this new thing that we don't understand as 'bad' quite quickly. Then, once we've seen an article in the paper supporting our viewpoint, the deal is sealed as far as we are concerned and we've decided that we'll never use it. Case closed. If anyone ever starts talking about it, then we'll confidently state that it's a bad thing and it's not worth getting involved with, thereby compounding the problem.

This is the normal response, by which I mean if you were to take a large group of people and explain Bitcoin to them, this would be the most common reaction. I know this because I get this response quite regularly when I'm talking to people about it. It's understandable, but it's also a very real obstacle to adoption. This is nicely demonstrated with a couple of interesting statistics; look how fast Uber became the world's largest taxi firm, with somewhere around 75 million customers, without even owning any taxis. Airbnb became the world's largest lodging company, without actually owning any actual places to stay, but with approximately 150 million users. How was this possible when Bitcoin, which is older than both of these companies, is still sitting on a miserly 20 odd million users?

Well, I don't know about you, but I can explain Uber quite easily as most people are familiar with taking a taxi. I can also explain Airbnb as most people have stayed in hotels or BnB's in their lifetimes. I can do that in one sentence actually. Bitcoin … not so much. And therein lies the problem.

The reality is that this won't change. It can't because Bitcoin is, simply, Bitcoin. This is not just new money, it's a new *concept*. It requires an entire book like this to explain it in detail. In short, this is not going to be easy. In fact, I can give you an example of just how difficult this can be.

Recently I took my car into a garage owned by an old school friend of mine. We have known each other since we were ten years old and we've seen each other's lives unfold. He knows I am passionate about technology, I know he loves cars, but in many ways our lives are worlds apart. During this particular visit, we'd talked a bit about what I was doing now as I'd recently sold a business and I explained that I had gone full time in cryptocurrency in general and Bitcoin in particular. He'd heard of it, but didn't understand it and had absolutely no interest in it, laughingly stating "If it ain't got the queen's head on it, mate, I'm not interested!"

Of course, no man is a prophet in his own land, but even so, I thought I might have been the one who was able to explain it succinctly to him, especially as I had some apparent credibility on the matter. It was not to be, but I liked his response as it sort of neatly summarized the problem very nicely – there's just too much information to cover too quickly to make it easily understandable, so we revert only to what we know. This is going to take some time, perhaps *a lot* of time. Is it possible it might be *too much* time and Bitcoin won't last the distance? It's a fair question.

These are all interesting points, but they don't cover the really big issues that Bitcoin has to overcome to succeed, and there probably three big ones that potentially have the power to derail the whole thing completely: governments, banks and, perhaps ironically, the environment.

We already know that (most) governments don't like it for reasons we've covered. If we exclude the ones that are either tolerating or supporting it, then we have to consider how the remaining ones are likely to react. Most of these are still a little on the fence, probably watching to see what other countries do first.

Some are actively exploring how they could work with it, others are not. But here's the key point – they ALL have the power, in theory, to stop it dead in its tracks.

In truth, this move almost certainly wouldn't completely succeed for reasons we've seen, but it could certainly make life very, very difficult for adoption. They could pass legislation making it illegal to own, trade or exchange into fiat money for example. It would be impossible to police the first one, difficult to do the second as there will probably always be a country or territory somewhere who will accept it, but relatively easy to do the third, and some countries have already done this. The effect has been that exchanges have simply moved somewhere else and provided an uninterrupted service. However, if enough of the 'first world' countries got together and agreed a universal ban forcing exchanges elsewhere, users might think twice about exchanging fiat money for Bitcoin in countries that have less than perfect trust ratings.

Banks also have some power here. They've already made life a little difficult in many places, but they could easily up their game if the threat became real, that is, adoption started gaining traction. They are, in many cases, the gateway to cryptocurrency, so what if they simply closed the gate? What if they collectively revoked all access to banking facilities for anyone involved in cryptocurrency in any way, whether individual, company or institution? Who's to stop them?

Well, the answer to that might be simply the will of the people together. If enough people are using it, believe in it and want it to succeed, this would be extremely difficult for the banks to do and a very unpopular move. The collective power of the people is a force to be reckoned with if you're on the wrong side of. But it works both ways and there's one element of Bitcoin that may well find itself *on* that wrong side – the environmental impact.

At first, this doesn't make sense. There are no banks guzzling power, there are no printing presses for 'Bitcoin' notes or mining (in the traditional sense) for metals to turn into Satoshi coins. There aren't even any large security trucks spurting out greenhouse gases delivering the stuff around the world, so how can there be such a concern over environmental impact? The answer is one word – electricity. Bitcoin needs A LOT of it.

For several (quite technical) reasons, it's quite hard to work out exactly how much power is being used by the Bitcoin network, but by any measure it's a staggering amount. Alex de Vries, a Bitcoin specialist at PricewaterhouseCoopers (PwC for short) carried out some research in mid-2018 to try and get some realistic numbers which were a bit more accurate than 'a lot'. He worked out that the *minimum* the network can be using is around 2.55 Gigawatts which is roughly 22 terawatt hours (TWh) per year. Of course, this is not something I can present to my mum because it doesn't mean anything to any of us on its own, so we need some context. Put it this way, Bitcoin almost certainly consumes more power than the entire country of Morocco. Or Iceland. Or Serbia, Hungary, Syria, Cuba, Slovenia, Slovakia, Bahrain. Even Ireland. In fact, if 'Bitcoin mining' was a country it would be ranked 61st in the world for electricity consumption. This is fine if it's all coming from renewable energy and the world has all the power it needs whenever it needs it, but we know that both of these things aren't true. It's definitely a concern.

I've written articles about why this may not be such an issue in the long term (as miners receive less reward over time) and the positives about people, in search of better profits, who are now encouraged to find cleaner, cheaper power for the benefit of all, but right now it may be enough of a problem to cause a global backlash. There are those that point out that banks and other financial systems use far more than this (which they do) but the reality is that Bitcoin is unlikely to actually replace the banking system, which means you are adding this power requirement to the world rather than replacing what already exists. Some countries have already taken steps to restrict access to surplus clean energy that Bitcoin operations have been traditionally drawn to because it's cheap, or ban operations completely, but as we already know that just moves the problem elsewhere. This is one of those issues that is bubbling under at the moment and could build into a powerful movement to slow it down, affecting the network behind Bitcoin. We shall see.

But even this list of problems isn't exhaustive. For some, the fact that it wasn't as anonymous as they thought it was is an issue. For others, the lack of a single point of leadership is a negative rather than a positive due to the time it takes to get a consensus from the myriad of people involved in the project. Then, there's the fact that most of the world is not yet accepting it (directly anyway) and negative press seems to be everywhere stopping that from happening.

Even those who use it acknowledge that there are other potential limitations aside from the speed and level of anonymity. For example, when transferring money to someone's bank account from your own using the traditional banking system, there are often checks in place to ensure that you've typed the sort code and account number correctly to begin with. Even if you've got it wrong and have sent the funds to the wrong place, you have some protection in place. This is especially true since the voluntary code on this issue that exists between banks in the UK was enhanced in January 2016, although it's interesting to note there was almost no recourse to reclaim if you made a mistake in a transfer before 2014. There's still no guarantees, of course, but the practical reality is that most incorrect payments are returned. When sending Bitcoin, there's no central authority to appeal to, so if it goes to the wrong place, it's almost certainly lost for good, even though you can see it on the blockchain.

And it's quite easy to do. Here's my Bitcoin address for example:

1LC1Nz6gk8u33qxVw9zuFvrzkXqc34EdwK

Imagine typing that out by hand! You're bound to get it wrong somewhere, so addresses are usually copied and pasted or done via other means (such as QR codes on phones) to make sure they're right. It isn't a foolproof system though, so for the time being caution – and lots of double checking - is key.

Finally, the cryptocurrency community hasn't helped itself either, creating new versions of Bitcoin, called 'Bitcoin Cash', 'Bitcoin Gold', 'Bitcoin Green', 'Bitcoin Diamond' and even, perhaps inevitably, 'Bitcoin Adult' amongst many others. Each proclaims to be the real interpretation of Satoshi Nakamoto's original white paper vision, like a bunch of religious factions arguing amongst each other over the finer detail of a holy manuscript and doing more damage collectively as a result.

These new 'coins' by the way, don't have any real value (even in the world of cryptocurrency) and are generally not seen as serious contenders for Bitcoin's crown, but they do confuse new people coming into the cryptocurrency market for the first time. Imagine, as a brand new user, being confronted with around 26 types of Bitcoin, 25 of which are next to worthless, when you go to buy some. How does that help anyone? This is the disadvantage of open source in that anyone can create a new coin and get it listed on various websites that are important to cryptocurrency nerds, but it doesn't mean anyone wants it or it has any value.

This will almost certainly sort itself out naturally in due course as the worthless versions wither and die, but in the meantime it works against adoption and makes life just that little bit harder for people wanting to be involved. At an early stage of development that can sometimes be enough to completely derail a project, at least for a while.

After having read these last two chapters, it's easy to see why there are so many people on both sides of the argument and why each person will usually stick to their side quite vehemently. The truth is that this is all completely speculative and entirely new – we just don't know for sure what will happen.

We're just going to have to wait and see.

Chapter 17

What Bitcoin can do for the world

"Bitcoin is the most important invention in the history of the world since the Internet."

– Roger Ver, Tech entrepreneur and business angel

If we ignore the 'will they, won't they' position we find ourselves in for the moment, it's fascinating to look at what a world using Bitcoin could look like. All these changes might be very painful to implement, so we have to ask ourselves if it's worth going through all the hassle to make it happen, or (like my mum would prefer) if we should stay in a world without it. Mind you, she also thinks that anything more modern than a video recorder is simply not necessary, but I kind of like being able to stream movies when I want them, so we'll have to agree to disagree on that one.

First, there are the simple cost savings it can produce and that can happen in two ways with Bitcoin's technology. As we've seen, moving traditional money about using traditional systems is expensive, but it's only when you look at the overall numbers you get a sense of just *how* expensive.

Annual world remittances (i.e. transfers) are probably somewhere around $700bn at the moment. There's some debate over this figure so let's not take it as gospel, just as an example. Out of this figure, banks and money transfer service providers will take their cut which, will usually be between 4% and 10%, either directly by fees or by providing a less favourable foreign exchange rate. Bitcoin transactions, of course, are only subject to network fees which are considerably lower. Even just assuming a 3% difference (made up of a worst case scenario for Bitcoin and a best case scenario for traditional money) would yield a global saving to consumers of $21bn. A year. That's $21bn that goes back into the economy. Ironically, the poorest ten per cent of the world's population pay the highest fees for their remittances at the moment, so the savings to this group are far higher in proportionate terms. Bitcoin, for the first time in history, creates a level playing field between rich and poor in at least one area of finance, and that can only be a good thing.

But it's not just people sending money over borders where Bitcoin has a real edge. Visa and MasterCard provide a global network where local currencies can be accepted almost anywhere, but someone has to pay for those services and it's usually the companies employing them. When you buy your weekly shop and pay by card, Tesco's has to hand over a small cut to the card provider which varies by type of card. Credit cards, for example, are usually more expensive than debit cards and whilst each amount is small, the combined total runs into hundreds of billions - on trillions of dollars' worth of annual sales. The numbers start to get so big that they hurt your head at this point, but if we were all to use Bitcoin instead, the fees would be much lower globally, releasing another hundred billion or so back into the economy. Way back in 2013, a Goldman Sachs analyst worked out that fees ran at about $260 billion for every $10 trillion in global sales, which isn't bad when you consider the percentage. However, switch to Bitcoin using this example and it drops to around $104 billion. I like the smaller number better. Unless you're Visa or MasterCard of course, in which case your profits have just been wiped out.

People have also figured out that this public record – that blockchain we keep referring to – keeps an unequivocal, incorruptible record of everyone's transactions on it. Forever. This is not great if you're using Bitcoin for unscrupulous purposes, but what if you actually *wanted* your transactions monitored? There are actually more reasons for this than might be immediately obvious.

Let's say you're buying a house. You'll need to pay solicitor's fees, land registry fees, stamp duty fees and a whole host of others to register your new ownership in multiple official books and records - a sort of 'proof' that you have paid for and own this property. However, if you'd paid for your property in Bitcoin, and you were willing to identify which was your transaction on the blockchain, then no further actual official record keeping would be needed other than something pointing to where that transaction sits. The transaction cannot be reversed, removed or otherwise altered as long as Bitcoin exists somewhere in the world. These third parties and all their associated costs can be removed from the equation, for good.

This part goes beyond Bitcoin on its own and people have built new networks using Bitcoin's design and made it a bit cleverer. On *these* systems, you can make it so that your house transaction would only complete when the payment actually goes through. In fact, you could do the whole chain in one press of the key, cheaply and instantly, with all the pre-requisites that need to be ticked off (surveys, lending requirements etc.) done first as a requirement, or 'condition', of your payment going through. I told you these guys are smart. I really wasn't kidding.

We've already looked at convenience, the fact that you can send money across borders for little or no fee, no-one can freeze your assets or take your money, you don't have to trust a central body (who will definitely abuse that trust at some point) and it's much, much faster than traditional banking transfers, so I'm not going to repeat them in detail here, other than to recognise they do actually belong in this chapter as well. The more important stuff, the stuff that really makes the difference, in my view, is much more than simple cost savings. Bitcoin, genuinely, can change the world.

I'll acknowledge right off the bat that this is a bold statement, but I'm going to stand by it. Let me give you an example.

According to Statista.com (an online site that gathers up and presents statistical data from around the world) mobile phone ownership across the planet is now at around 4.6 billion people, or around 62% of the entire earth's population. Bloomberg, according to a report way back in 2012, puts it at 75%, so let's assume it's somewhere between the two for the purposes of this example.

At the same time, somewhere between 1.7 billion and 2.0 billion people have no access to banking facilities via any means at all. Whilst countries such as Denmark, Finland and Norway claim to have 100% of their population 'banked', some developing economies such as Pakistan, Iraq, Afghanistan, Chad and many, many others – especially in Africa - have less than 15% in the same category. There are some surprises too; huge economies like India and China are home to enormous amounts of unbanked people and there are well over a million unbanked people in Spain and the same in Germany, although probably for different reasons that exist in the developing world. The harsh reality is that it is just not profitable for the banking giants to provide services for people who are in remote areas, under corrupt governments or who don't have much money to start with. No profit = no service.

That said, the situation has been improving over the last few years, but an obvious and immediate solution presents itself when you compare the data for mobile phone penetration with access to bank accounts. Imagine, for example, giving a single smartphone to a remote village in Africa. Suddenly, they are not only connected to the rest of the world, but they also have their own entire bank. Through this bank, they can now interact with everyone else on the planet financially. They can buy, sell, send and receive money to and from anyone at any time, regardless of what their government says and without asking permission from any central banking authority who like to control these sorts of things. All for tiny amounts in terms of transaction fees (remember, the poorest people pay the highest fees for traditional money transfer services) and all in real time. This is a total game changer for people in this situation. The global playing field has just been levelled.

But that's not all. Think of all the global catastrophes that the world has faced (and will face again) and the difference a monetary system like Bitcoin could make. I am always impressed by mankind's ability to step in and help our global neighbours, despite our well-documented flaws that I haven't been shy about bringing up. Sadly, the truth is that this help, usually given in monetary format by governments or fundraisers of all sizes, is often lost in enormous administration fees, seized by corrupt governments or otherwise intercepted by local organised crime. No one knows just how much is lost through these channels, the only thing we do know for certain is that a significant percentage of it never makes it to where it was intended. Using Bitcoin, it's possible to bypass the suspect organisations who sit between those who donate and those who are supposed to receive that donation. This has never been possible until now.

What's even more exciting, is that everything that is required to make this work, in technological terms, is readily available *right now*. Yes, Bitcoin is still in its infancy, but this could be made to happen whenever we wanted. It could happen probably quite quickly with the will and blessing of the most powerful 1% on the planet but, as we've seen, this group stands to lose the most from relinquishing a sizeable portion of that central control, so it's unlikely to happen that way in reality. More likely, it'll come from the collective power of the people, over time, bypassing that 1% and forcing it through themselves.

Now I *do* sound like a total subversive. If I'm not careful, I'll find myself on a hit list somewhere.

And my mum wouldn't like that at all.

Chapter 18

What's next for Bitcoin?

"You can't stop things like Bitcoin. It will be everywhere and the world will have to readjust. World governments will have to readjust"

– John McAfee, Founder of McAfee Anti-Virus

For all the things we've talked about, the fact is that Bitcoin is just getting started. It is, truthfully speaking, an experiment that is barely out of the laboratory. Yet it really has already created enormous interest across all sectors of society and right across the world. Whatever happens from this point onwards, the world will never be the same. You simply can't put the genie back in the bottle.

Those of us who remember the start of the internet remember feeling the exact same thing as we're feeling now. There's excitement at the possibility that lays ahead, fear of the problems it may bring and more people than ever saying it'll never work. Actually, it probably only *seems* like there are more people saying it will never work because the reality is that it is so much easier now than it was thirty years ago to voice an opinion. That'll be thanks to the internet. Y'know, the very thing that they said wouldn't work in the first place. Oh, the irony.

We really do stand at a point where the world is going to change and the point of momentum has already been passed. However, there's a lot of work to be done and a whole load of problems to solve, many of which we probably don't even know we don't know yet. If you were comparing Bitcoin and cryptocurrency to the internet, we're probably in 1994 right now.

If you weren't there, let me remind you what it was like. Whilst those of us who were using the internet back then were already terribly excited about it, the fact is when you look back, it was horrible. The only way you could connect was by unplugging your (land line) phone and plugging in another cable that came from your computer to the same socket and enduring a screeching noise for around a minute as it made a connection to a server somewhere. Then, it allowed you – extremely slowly – to access text-based websites using very early browsers like Mosaic and Netscape, neither of which exist today. Updating websites was also difficult so information was often out of date, assuming you could find it in the first place since search engines were next to useless. There were no smartphones and Wi-Fi was just a weird word that someone made up.

There was no video, no streaming services and no way to easily shop online, but there was also no shortage of scepticism over its actual use beyond certain geeky applications because of these obvious limitations. The bottom line was that only people who understood that it was in its infancy could really see the potential, which is exactly where cryptocurrencies are now. But even early adopters (myself included) could not have imagined the impact that social media (Facebook, Twitter, Instagram, Snapchat and the like) would have or the applications that the third generation of development would bring, such as Airbnb and Uber. It took twenty years for that to really get going, whereas Bitcoin has only been around for ten so far and it's only very recently that it has started to gain real traction. The brain power that is being applied now across the world is unprecedented, even by the standards set by the development of the internet.

I remember talking to my geeky friends one day in 1995 and finding it was possible to send a fax from a computer using a long string of code. This wasn't using the internet of course, because it didn't exist in the format we know today at that time and we weren't connected to it anyway, but there were a series of interconnected computer systems that you could send a bit of code by if you knew how. I could type my message in quotation marks, add in the fax number, tell the computer network how to route it with a command line and press the enter key.

Excited by this and using what I'd learned, I sent the message "Hi Dad, call me when you get this" to my dad's number (he was the only one I knew who had a fax machine) and waited for the call. Two days later, he rang me asking why I'd sent it. It had taken that long to get there – technically slower than a first-class letter - but I thought it was really cool. My dad, on the other hand, wasn't terribly impressed by my technological prowess, even though he didn't have email or internet or even a mobile phone and this was the first time he'd received a message electronically, albeit printed on a piece of paper.

Using Bitcoin today is a bit like me sending that fax in 1995 – clunky, time-consuming and not completely user-friendly. But we no longer send messages that way and we barely even use fax machines anymore. Compare that to how we communicate today; we throw a message together on a touch-sensitive screen and send it via email, WhatsApp, Messenger, Skype, text or any other number of instant, easy systems without a second thought. We are able to get an instant response or even see each other when we're speaking, no matter where we are in the world. Gone are the long lines of code and knowledge of how to route a message, because it's all done in the background – automatically – for you. No-one could have imagined that level of ease in 1995, even nerds like me.

This, of course, is what using Bitcoin will be like before we even know it. The technology is being developed as I type these words and it's only a matter of time before it's fully integrated into existing platforms and systems, making it user-friendly for everyone. I'm not holding my breath for my mum getting involved though.

That part is relatively easy, actually. We've already built global platforms and systems, so we know for sure we can do that. The really tricky parts will come from working out how to regulate it, how to store it safely and how to stop it being so volatile, all of which are recognised - even if we're some way off the answers yet. This is all assuming that governments and banks don't try and stop it, of course.

Right now, it's a classic chicken-and-egg scenario. Because, in relative terms, such a small number of people are using it, the pressure to resolve these (non-technical) issues is arguably lower. But without proper legislation and a clear way to work with it, many people are put off using it and institutions can't include it in their portfolios. At some point, the balance will change one way or the other and the way forward will become clearer. We're just not there yet.

One thing is for sure; using Bitcoin tomorrow is going to be very different from using Bitcoin today. In the same way my own children can't imagine a world without the internet, I wonder if theirs will be able to imagine a world without Bitcoin?

Chapter 19

It's Bitcoin, but not as we know it

"[Bitcoin] is working. There may be other currencies like it that may be even better. But in the meantime, there's a big industry around Bitcoin."

— Sir Richard Branson, Founder of Virgin Group

Bitcoin is the first 'real' de-centralised cryptocurrency the world has ever seen, but it certainly hasn't been the last. Since its creation, there have been thousands of new coins generated because, once someone has done it and put that clever bit of code out there, anyone can do it. And they most certainly have!

Most of these coins are utterly worthless. Of those, some are genuine but have no use, some are well-meaning, but won't succeed, some are no more than a joke that got out of hand, and some are downright out-and-out scams designed to do no more than to part you from your cash. It all sounds quite scary from the outside, but actually, applying common sense and doing even some basic research can avoid any pitfalls if you're careful. Most people, including myself, think there will only ever be a handful of currencies in the long term (and perhaps not even *that* many) but whatever happens we almost certainly won't need the two thousand odd that exist right now.

Remember, Bitcoin itself is very old now in technical terms. Each time a new coin has been created it has been made better than its predecessor, although I'd argue none are perfect. Because things are changing so fast, it's actually possible that the coin that becomes the 'world standard' (if that even actually happens) may well not even have been created yet.

The reason I created this chapter was simply to introduce you, albeit briefly, to a couple of the other cryptocurrencies out there that have significant recognition in the industry to some extent. You may or may not come across them, but next time you find yourself in a conversation about cryptocurrencies (!) you will know some of the names that are being thrown about.

ETHEREUM
Technically not a currency (although it can be used as one) but one of those very clever systems we talked about earlier where you can

make transactions conditional on certain things happening first – known as a 'smart contract'. A genius piece of work that broke new ground for the technology, although many people now think the third generation systems will be better and faster.

RIPPLE

A system designed purely to work with the banks and ultimately replace the archaic SWIFT system for moving money around the globe instantly and very cheaply. It has a huge following, and already has partnerships with most large-scale banks. However, it is often criticised for not being a true cryptocurrency due to the way it operates.

LITECOIN

Designed to be 'silver' to Bitcoin's 'gold', Litecoin is four times faster than Bitcoin and was created to fill the gaps where paying with Bitcoin would be impractical, such as the coffee shop example. It's a solid, genuine coin, but some people question its value in the long term as newer coins supersede it.

BITCOIN CASH

A much faster version of the original Bitcoin, formed by a group who wanted to create a sleeker, more modern Bitcoin, solving many problems of the original. It's great in theory (although it creates confusion through its name) but it simply does not have the community behind it and may well be made obsolete anyway if the Lightning Network succeeds. Bitcoin Cash recently splintered into separate factions who are still infighting and may even completely destroy itself.

EOS

One of the different versions of Ethereum mentioned previously designed to create a way to run the smart contracts. Much newer and, as yet, unproven, it has gained quite a following.

MONERO
A completely private version of Bitcoin, where it is all but impossible to trace transactions. This has gained popularity over the last year or so and most people think it has a future in a world where you want to hide your transactions, a real digital version of 'cash' in many ways.

DOGECOIN
Created purely and simply as a joke coin way back in the early days of cryptocurrency, its level of adoption was so great that it became a legend in its own right. Today, it is still in the top 25 list of cryptocurrencies even without any development or apparent future. The community, in a permanent tongue in cheek way, simply continues to support it because, well, it's funny.

NEO
Another of the new 'smart contract' platforms that has gathered a lot of attention recently, sometimes for the wrong reasons. It's entirely unproven, like most of its colleagues, but promises a great deal on successful implementation – assuming that ever happens.

TETHER
A controversial 'stable coin' designed to create a way in which to keep money in the cryptocurrency market without actually holding any. The idea is that every Tether (always worth $1) is backed by a real dollar bill in the bank and you can simply swap between Tether and other currencies when you want to. However, there has been doubt as to whether this is actually the case and some suspicion over the motives of the people issuing Tether in the first place, reducing its credibility.

The problem with creating a list like this is that it will always raise the "why didn't you include (insert coin name here)?" question. I could have mentioned other 'privacy coins' (similar to Monero listed above) such as Dash, Zcash and Pivx, or other 'smart contract' platforms such as Lisk, Cardano and Qtum, or even more joke coins such as Garlic Coin, Useless Ethereum Token or Whopper Coin but the point of this list was simply to introduce the fact that there are currencies other than Bitcoin.

For reasons we have now been through, it's very hard to determine what the future of any of these coins are, especially when we can't even be certain about Bitcoin itself. No-one questions the advances in technology that some of the groups behind these coins are making, but history has shown us that quite often the advances made don't always work the first time around, more often than not being mere building blocks for the next generation of technology that takes off. This could well be the case here and until the dust settles a bit, we (i.e., those of us who are on the outside of this development work) are going to have to wait and see how it unfolds.

That said, I'm happy to go on record to say that I don't think we'll be buying coffees in the high street with Trump Coin, Spankcoin or Insanecoin anytime soon.

And you can take *that* to the bank.

Chapter 20

So, what do I do now?

"Don't limit your child to your own learning, for he was born in another time."

– Rabindranath Tagore, Artist, musician, poet

Well, that's up to you!

The objective of writing this book was simply to achieve the goal written on the front of it – to explain Bitcoin to my mum, and, by extension, anyone who wanted to get the basics down in a simple way. Put it this way: it's a book I would have *loved* to have had access to when starting my own cryptocurrency journey. Where you go from here depends on how you feel about it now that you understand it a little more.

You might have a sudden desire to go out and get some Bitcoin. If you do, that's great, and don't forget to claim your free Bitcoin to get you started by following the instructions at the back of this book. If you don't, that's ok too. The point is, you know enough now to be able to make that decision properly.

But it *is* true to say that none of us really know how this will play out. We all have our own hopes and agendas of course, and those of us who saw the internet unfold before our very eyes can't help but feel it's the same thing all over again – just bigger and better. It could well be that Bitcoin does to the financial sector what email did for the postal service, but it could also be a global experiment that will fail, only for the ashes to be the foundation of the next generation of cryptocurrency. Two things are for certain: one, whatever happens from this point, Bitcoin is already part of global history, and two, there will *definitely* be some form of global digital currency in the future in some format or another.

In my view, it will take no more than another couple of years from now to have a good indication of where we're going with this. By then, the position on regulation should be clearer, the technology winners and losers should be emerging and institutions will either be heavily involved, fuelling new development, or forced out of the market altogether by legislation in their countries. Until then, it's worth keeping a casual eye on financial media (the mainstream and tabloid media aren't terribly good at getting their facts right on this subject) and watching the story unfold, or follow key advocates and commentators such as Andreas Antonopoulos, Charlie Shrem and Brian Armstrong. These guys *really* know their stuff.

Unsurprisingly, there are many books on the subject, some good, some bad, and I keep a list of works I am happy to recommend to people who would like to know more on my cryptocurrency blog site at www.originalcryptoguy.com. Simply go to that site, select 'Books by Jason' at the top of the page and then the title of this book to find them.

For now, whatever your position on Bitcoin is, I'd like to thank you for taking the time to understand it. It really is an important thing to do and it puts you well inside the top 1% of the planet in terms of knowledge. That's a very privileged position.

And for me, next time I drop in to see my mum, she will, hopefully, be able to understand what I'm talking about before she says the same thing that all mums say the world over when their adult son drops in:

"That sounds nice, dear. Would you like a cup of tea?"

Claim your FREE Bitcoin!

If you're ready to join the world of cryptocurrency, then it's time to claim your free Bitcoin! Not a whole one you understand, but enough to get you started!

First, you'll need to create a wallet to store your Bitcoin and I've prepared a nice easy guide on how to do that on my website. Simply go to www.originalcryptoguy.com and from the main header select 'Books by Jason' and then the title of this book. In the section below there is a link to the illustrated guide. Don't worry, it's very simple and isn't that much different from setting up an email address. Once you've done this, you'll be able to use this wallet for all your transactions in the future if you want to.

Once you've done that, follow the instructions to get the address I'll need to send it to, a bit like sending someone your sort code and account number to do a direct bank transfer. It will look something like this:

1LC1Nz6gk8u33qxVw9zuFvrzkXqc34EdwK

Copy the address, taking care to ensure that you have all of it, and then go to the 'contact' section on my website. Fill in your name and email address where indicated and then, in the section market 'comment', paste your Bitcoin address along with the date you purchased your copy of the book and where you bought it from (e.g. Amazon, Lulu.com etc.). I will process your Bitcoin claim as soon as I am able but please allow up to ten days to receive it. I will email you when it is done.

Incidentally, it's quite safe to give out your public Bitcoin address and you'll always need to when receiving Bitcoin, but no one will be able to access your funds. It's a bit like giving out your email address

– someone can use it to send you an email but they can't get access to your email account.

However, you must never give out your keys or twelve-word passcode (you get these when you set up your wallet) to anyone at any time, even if they claim they need it for something (they don't). This is like handing over your bank card and PIN number!

Enjoy your Bitcoin!

And finally ...

This book is intended to be a gentle, yet extensive, introduction to Bitcoin and there are some very technical areas I have not addressed. If you have any questions about Bitcoin that you feel I haven't covered, or have general feedback on the book itself, you can get in touch via the 'contact' page at www.originalcryptoguy. com

<u>Sources:</u>

I have read hundreds, if not thousands, of articles on Bitcoin and watched many hours of related videos over the last few years to find the information both for this book and my blog pieces on www.originalcryptoguy.com

There are too many to mention in terms of general information, but where specific data is needed, I have researched this online, usually cross-referencing across several sources, and then credited the appropriate work here.

"The world's 2 billion unbanked, in 6 charts", Business Insider Report, August 30th 2017

"Financial Inclusion on the Rise, But Gaps Remain, Global Findex Database Shows" Worldbank.org Press Release, April 19th 2018

"How Bitcoin is changing the world", Andreas Antonopoulos, Internetdagarna 2017

"Bitcoin: A Peer-to-Peer Electronic Cash System", Satoshi Nakamoto, 2008

"Introduction to Bitcoin", Andreas Antonopoulos, Singularity University's Innovation Partnership Program (IPP) Presentation, 2016

"Nearly 4 Million Bitcoins Lost Forever, New Study Says", Fortune.com, November 25th 2017

"Man who 'threw away' Bitcoin now worth over $80m wants to dig up landfill site", The Independent, 4th December 2017

"Countries Where Bitcoin Is Legal & Illegal", Investopedia, October 11th 2018

"How Many People Use Bitcoin in 2018?", Bitcoin Market Journal, 31st July 0218

"Number of Bitcoin ATMs worldwide from January 2016 to October 2018", Satista.com, October 2018

"Here's how much money there is in the world — and why you've never heard the exact number", Business Insider, 17th November 2011

"Brief 9 (2014): Bitcoin and other cryptocurrencies", HMRC, March 2014

"Porn Sites Get More Visitors Each Month than Netflix, Amazon and Twitter Combined", Huffington Post, May 2013

"Bill Gates: I would short bitcoin if I could", CNBC, 7th May 2018

"Bitcoin will someday be worth as much as 40 times its current value, says Cameron Winklevoss", CNBC, 7th February 2018

"Warren Buffett says bitcoin is 'probably rat poison squared'", CNBC, 5th May 2018

"Dr. Nouriel Roubini vs. Bitcoin: Senate Hearing Breaks Down His Arguments", Yahoo Finance, 11th October 2018

"Paul Krugman's Poor Prediction", Lapham's Quarterly, undated

"Bitcoin Obituaries", 99bitcoins.com (constantly updated)

"Why Bitcoin uses so much energy", The Economist, 9th July 2018

"Bitcoin Mining Now Consuming More Electricity than 159 Countries Including Ireland & Most Countries in Africa", Powercompare.com, November 2017

"New study quantifies bitcoin's ludicrous energy consumption", arstechnica.com, 17th May 2018

Coin valuations obtained from coinmarketcap.com, October 2018

Additional statistical data obtained from Statista.com, October 2018

Author's disclosure:
Jason holds a substantial cryptocurrency portfolio both in direct holdings and via CFDs (Contracts for Difference) including Bitcoin, Litecoin, Ripple, Ethereum, Monero, Stellar, Neo, EOS, Cardano, IOTA, OMG, BAT, Golem, Status, Funfair, Salt, Civic, Storj and Aragon.

Disclaimer:
All the views in this book are those of the author and in no way constitute financial or investment advice. If this book has inspired you to get involved with investments in the cryptocurrency space, it is very important that you do your own research first.

Also by the same author

Do you and your partner avoid talking about money?
Do one, or both of you, think the other spends too much?
Does it feel like you're not in control of your money?
You're not alone!

Most of us are *terrible* at communicating about money with
our partners and this can cause problems. Whether it's
dealing with debt, secret spending or simply no idea whether
you're really moving forward as a couple, the result can be
stress, frustration or arguments.
If this sounds familiar, this book is the answer! Its proven
system has been devised over many years of helping couples
and families in all financial situations – both good and bad -
get control of their money.

Using the **FREE PRE-PROGRAMMED SPREADSHEETS** it
comes with, you'll follow a step by step process to make order
from chaos, learn how to communicate about money openly
and, finally, work towards the financial goals you set together.
Welcome to Perfect Financial Balance!

Available in eBook and paperback on Amazon, Lulu.com &
www.originalcryptoguy.com

www.ingramcontent.com/pod-product-compliance
Lightning Source LLC
Chambersburg PA
CBHW071435180526
45170CB00001B/355